# BEATEN, BUT UNBOWED

Waking from the nightmare of abuse

KAREN BRAYSHER

RED
LETTER
BOOKS

Designed and produced in Great Britain, 2017 by
Red Letter Books Ltd
Bay Tree Cottage
Fletching
East Sussex  TN22 3TA

www.redletterbooks.co.uk

Ghostwritten with Hannah Sherriffs
Typeset in Garamond by Red Letter Books Ltd
Printed by CreateSpace

# INVICTUS

OUT of the night that covers me,
Black as the Pit from pole to pole,
I thank whatever gods may be
For my unconquerable soul.
In the fell clutch of circumstance
I have not winced nor cried aloud.
Under the bludgeonings of chance
My head is bloody, but unbowed.
Beyond this place of wrath and tears
Looms but the Horror of the shade,
And yet the menace of the years
Finds, and shall find, me unafraid.
It matters not how strait the gate,
How charged with punishments the scroll,
I am the master of my fate:
I am the captain of my soul.

**WILLIAM ERNEST HENLEY (1849–1903)**

# FOREWORD

THIS is an extremely courageous book. I believe that the courage it took to write it grew not only from Karen's experiences, but from how she has chosen to face everything that has happened to her and her beloved sister, Lorraine with unflinching truthfulness and the very opposite of self-pity.

Karen's account is not a misery memoir. It is full of warmth and humour. She is not a victim, but a survivor. Many of us have stories to tell, but few would be as vivid or honest as this one.

Karen asked me to write these few words because we met when she became a Service User Governor at the NHS trust at which I was then Chief Executive. We have since become friends, and she has been a great support to me as I have tentatively begun to talk about my own experiences of mental illness. But she also asked me to introduce her story because, long ago, I was a staff nurse at Chailey Heritage where I knew her sister, Lorraine and I looked after some of the other children who lived there and were also very badly affected by thalidomide.

The full and devastating impact of this drug on children and their families was hidden for many years. It didn't 'just' cause absence or serious deformities of arms, legs, hands and feet. Depending on how early in pregnancy it was taken, thalidomide also damaged the development of the baby's internal organs, eyes and ears. Children were born with cleft lips and palates, twisted intestines, holes in the heart, damaged kidneys, lack of skin pigmentation, deafness and blindness.

But there was worse cruelty. Bonding with a baby doesn't come naturally to all mothers and fathers; some parents have to work harder at it than others. If the child has a disability, this can get in the way of bonding. Lack of bonding can lie at the root of future mental illness for a child who does not feel loved. Back in the late 1950s/early 1960s, it was the fashion for some doctors to advise parents who gave birth to a disabled child to place them in institutional care. They were told to forget about them and go on to have another 'normal' child. Add this to the secrecy and shame that surrounded the children affected by thalidomide, and the disgraceful cover-up over many decades by the company that produced the drug, and you have a recipe for alienation and abuse.

Karen and Lorraine have somehow found the strength to rise above such difficult beginnings. Their deep attachment and affection for one another and Karen's journey to learn to love herself is very moving. I hope that many people will read this book and be inspired by their story of survival and love.

LISA RODRIGUES CBE, MARCH 2017

WE all have a story inside us. Likewise, events and people in our lives form our memories, good and bad. My memories are so graphic that they have haunted my mind for a long time. During the writing of this book I have had to relive abuse, abandonment, guilt and the consequences of my bipolar and dyslexia. It has been a painful experience, but necessary for me to heal and move forward positively. Self-hate to self-love has been my reward.

I now appreciate that it was my spirit which protected me, and made me the survivor I was and still am today.

I would like to dedicate this book to Lorraine, my marvellous sister, and to my wonderful friends who provide me with all the support I need.

N.B: This is a true story. But some people's names, and details about them, have been changed.

KAREN BRAYSHER, MARCH 2017

# CONTENTS

# REPLACEMENT BABY

## Cuckfield Hospital, 1961

IT was a forceps delivery. How else would you deliver a breach baby with no arms or legs?

Lorraine was quickly wrapped up in a blanket and taken to an incubator. Everyone was stunned. No one had seen such a baby before, only heard about them.

My father, Reg, was called for and my mother, Brenda, was sedated.

"I'm afraid your daughter probably won't live for more than 48 hours, Mr Braysher," the doctor told Dad.

I am sitting with Dad in the kitchen and he is telling me the story of Lorraine's birth. The house is quiet because my mother has taken Lorraine on a week's holiday to the Thalidomide Trust's hotel in Jersey. It is peaceful, and he is peaceful. This moment will be my happiest teenage memory; one of the best memories of my whole childhood, in fact. I am so content – just me and Dad. As we used to be.

"The doctor asked if I'd like to see her," continues Dad, his voice soft. "So I followed the nurse into the baby ward and looked down at my tiny new daughter. I could only see her face as she was bundled up in blankets (she was so pretty that later on she adopted the name 'Dolly'). There seemed to be nothing wrong with her. But then, of course, when I pulled back the blanket she looked like something out of the freak tent at the circus."

He puts his head in his hands. "I couldn't believe how she looked. It was so completely shocking. There was no way I was going to tell your mother at that stage – we didn't think she'd live, so why bother saying anything?"

"Did you know what was wrong with her?" I ask, curious to

know if thalidomide birth defects were instantly recognised.

"We had no idea. We certainly didn't realise there were thousands of families going through the same thing. Although I must have made some kind of connection, because when your mother was pregnant with you they had her in hospital with drugs going in intravenously against morning sickness and I got her out. I told the doctor, 'We've already had one disabled child – we'll not have another.'

"But back then, I went round to see Auntie Gill [Mum's middle sister] after I'd seen Lorraine for the first time.

'Boy or girl?' she asked.

'Girl,' I said.

'Oh wonderful!' said your auntie.

'No, Gill, she's all buggered up! We're starting to prepare for her funeral.'

And when Lorraine stayed alive, there was no question of her coming home with us to Haywards Heath. She was taken to Chailey Heritage to be looked after and the doctor said to us, 'Forget about this one, Mr Braysher. Just go home and have another.' So, that's where you come in, Annie, 13 months later – our 'replacement' baby," he says, smiling at me.

He has not called me 'Annie' for so long. It was the name he used when I was little – his 'little Princess Annie'. Anne is my middle name, after Princess Anne. Mum and my elder sister, Sue, would call me 'Awkward Annie' (and still think I am just awkward rather than ill), but never Dad. I was always his 'Princess', until I hit my teenage years when I became plain 'Karen' to him.

# FINGERS AND TOES

"THE first thing I did when you were brought to me," my mother told me, "was to count every finger on your hands and every toe on your feet, just to make sure you were all there. You might have been born with the cord round your neck, but apart from that you were fine."

There was relief all round. I was their final child – their fourth – and, as a replacement for Lorraine, I was thankfully perfectly formed. However, it was not my digits my mother should have been concerned about. I was to become disabled in a less obvious way, which remained undiagnosed for over forty years, and it was both the making of me, and the breaking of me.

Unfortunately, the relationship with my mother was the first to break down, even before my mental health sealed its fate. When I look back at photographs of her and me as a child, there is no love there. There is one of us sitting on the bed, seemingly for a bedtime story, and I am pointing at the book which is lying on the bed clothes and she perches awkwardly next to me. There is no contact between us, no cuddling or even touching of shoulders. She is as I remember her – very cold and disinterested in me. I am more trouble than I am worth. She pulls me along, aggressive in action and words, when we are out shopping. I am always making her late, or dragging her down. I am too much of a tomboy, too naughty, too awkward, too rude; the list is endless.

We only visited Lorraine on Sunday afternoons when we were young, so I had no one to play with for most of the week and it was a lonely existence with older siblings who bossed me about and did not want to play. It was only our Collie dogs – Lassie and Bob – who would play with me. They lived outdoors because my mother did not like their hair in her immaculate house. I would occasionally help her do some baking, and I could watch *Blue Peter* because it was educational, but that was all my entertainment at home. I would repeatedly ask for Lorraine to be allowed to come home for longer, but she would always say, "I'm not having her home."

"Why not?" I would ask.

"Because Lorraine needs specialist care, and anyway it's none of your business."

Dad seemed to agree with Mum – probably because it would not have been him taking care of Lorraine.

But I kept asking for Lorraine. I missed my sister and I knew she missed me too, even though she had her own 'brothers and sisters' at Chailey Heritage – the Thalidomiders were (and still are) a close-knit group.

To add to my feeling of loneliness, I remember our mother would calmly and repeatedly tell me that she wished neither Lorraine nor I had survived. "You were born with the cord around your neck, Karen. It's a pity it didn't strangle you at birth. I wish I'd never had the two of you. We were happy before you both came along, and you've been more trouble than everybody else put together."

Our mother did have a point, I suppose, in that Lorraine's disability was plain to see; of course, our mother had to make an effort the rare times when Lorraine was at home. But me? I apparently deserved everything I got. Which was a lot. She had no tolerance for cheek, naughtiness, untidiness or normal childish behaviour. I spent a lot of time crying after I had been smacked or slapped by her. At that point, it was only ever her, never Dad, and she never hit me in front of him.

It always made me wonder, why did she bother to have us, anyway, when she had seemingly had it so easy with David and Sue, our elder siblings.

Auntie Gill provided me with a possible answer when I was cutting her hair many years later. "I think your mother was jealous of me, Karen." I stopped, my scissors hanging in the air. This was the part of my job I enjoyed the most: hearing stories… especially those about my family.

"What do you mean, she was jealous?" I replied.

"Well, your mum had Sue and David already; they must have

been around seven and eight when we went on a camping holiday. I was heavily pregnant at the time and your mother turned to me and said, 'I could have another baby, you know.'

'Really?' I said to her, 'Are you seriously thinking about it?'

She said nothing more, but I did think it was strange for her to be wanting to have another baby. Why would she want to go through all that bringing up a baby again? The only thing I could think of was that she had been so young when she had them, in her late teens, she now felt jealous of me. Either way, next time I saw her she declared she was pregnant."

"How strange," I said, without thinking. "She'd had it soooo easy with David and Sue." I could feel the familiar bile rising. "The blue-eyed children, never causing her any problems – sailed through life, they did," I spat venomously. "No wonder she wanted us dead."

"Perhaps she just had less tolerance with you two – she was an older mum by that time," replied Auntie Gill, trying to defuse my anxiety.

"I don't know why you defend her," I said, angrily slashing my scissors through the air. "You hate her – or you certainly did."

"I don't hate your mother, Karen. I think she's selfish and she always has been – I've already told you stories about her."

# POLES APART

AUNTIE Gill, my mother and my other four aunties grew up on a very poor council estate in Haywards Heath, in Bencewood Cresent which was then the worst road in town. Times were hard post-War, and they were made even harder by their nasty, brutish bully of a father – my grandfather, Jack Stubbings. He was in the Home Guard and was a gamekeeper, and also Rodent Officer for the Council. Another hair client of mine, Mrs Hayden, can remember repeatedly talking on the bus with my grandmother, Daisy. "Oh, she was a very put upon woman, Karen. Constantly cowed by her husband and weighed down by the demands of those Stubbings girls."

The sisters had hard lives and were forced to go out rabbiting with their father to catch food for the table. Auntie Gill, who is the most feminine woman I know, told me, "He used to dress us up as boys and we'd have to hold the net over the main hole while he sent the ferrets down other holes. This poor rabbit would bolt up from the burrow, get caught in the net and be attacked by the ferret. I'll never forget the rabbit shrieking. The worst part was then having to go home and eat the rabbit in a stew. Every mouthful was upsetting to me."

There was never enough food to go round and, in fact, there was never enough of anything to go around and that was why all my aunts remember my mother, the second eldest, as being particularly 'selfish'.

"She wouldn't share things with us," Auntie Daphne, the youngest, once told me. "I remember your mother tussling with Auntie Hazel over a dress. Hazel had borrowed your mum's dress, probably without asking, and your mother was furious – 'How dare you borrow this – it's mine', sort of thing. Their fight had moved from the bedroom onto the landing and there was now screaming and then blows. Hazel must have run down the stairs to tell on your mother, and Father came running up the stairs and got hold of your mother and kicked her down, and back up, the stairs. 'You have to share things in this house, Brenda!' he shouted after her. 'You can't be a selfish little bitch – we can't afford wardrobes full of dresses!' he added, walking by her slumped body." (They say violence never works – it certainly did not in my mother's case as it seemed to reinforce, rather than improve, her selfish nature.)

It comes as no surprise that the girls wanted to escape from their home life as soon as they could, and were all married young. My mother spotted her opportunity – with my father – and grabbed it.

They were at the same school and he was good-looking and from a smarter street in Haywards Heath, Allen Road. The Brayshers, with long links to the village of Bolney, were a much better class of family than the Stubbings.

Mrs Dollarmore, another of my hair clients, knew my father's family and told me about them. I feel such a connection to this side of my family. On the maternal side, there was Emma Remnant, my great grandmother. She was married to William, who was in the Veterinary Corps looking after War horses, and I remember her only as an old lady dressed in mourning clothes. In her time, she had run the laundry on the Hodgestone Estate and would wash the pub landlord's shirts and starch his collars, on the sly, in exchange for a pint of Guinness.

Their daughter, my Nan, Nellie, worked for many years as a daily maid for Lady Buxton in Lindfield High Street and they became good friends. Wedding photos show the Remnants to be immaculately well-dressed (you can tell by the shoes and ties) and Dad grew up with love all around him, from his mum and his Auntie Edie – such a happy childhood.

I also feel a particular connection to the males on the paternal side, because of their 'medical-type' tempers. My grandfather, Alfred, was a bricklayer and both my father and his brother, Ron, followed in his footsteps. Dad told me a typical tale about Alfred's mercurial anger. "After doing my first proper day's work, aged about 14, my new boss asked me what I wanted as payment. 'I quite like the trowel I've been using today, can I take that?' So, I came home, proudly carrying my new trowel. 'Look what I've got, Dad, as payment for today's work.' My father's face turned thunderous and he snatched it off me and threw it, while shouting 'Bloody trowel', right down to the bottom of the garden. I was quite upset about that and I spent hours searching for it in the brambles. It was the fact that my hard-won payment had been rejected. But Dad's erratic temper was legendary."

My father was not cowed by Alfred's moods, because he was a fighter and had spirit, but, unfortunately, the tempers (and other brain disorders, such as severe epilepsy) continued down the genetic line to my father and his brother's daughter. But it is reassuring, in a way, to know that there is some genetic basis to my bipolar.

It is obvious why my mother thought Dad was a catch. He had a stable, loving family and life would be comfortable with him. I do not know any details of their courtship, but I presume they got engaged after leaving school and married soon after, because David came along when our mother was 19.

In the meantime, Dad had a stroke of luck when Lady Buxton (who his mum worked for) overheard their conversation one coffee break while he was at the house doing some building maintenance.

"I need some money to invest in this Self-Help Building Scheme, Mother."

"Well, I'm afraid me and your dad can't give you that amount," replied Nellie. "We just don't have it."

"What's this about needing money, Braysher?" interrupted Lady Buxton.

"I want to build my own home under a Government scheme, but I need some money to get me started."

"I'll sponsor you," she said, without hesitation. She must have thought highly of my nan, and Dad, to offer such support and provide the means for Dad to take his first step towards becoming a Master Builder. It is no wonder that one of Nan's most cherished possessions was an oil painting of Lady Buxton's house. I rescued it from my mother's loft, ultimately saving it from the tip.

With Lady Buxton's help, Dad built his own house in Haywards Heath and he and my mother played happy families with David and Sue. According to my mother, it was when Lorraine and I came into the family that things went wrong for them all.

# TREEHOUSES AND SLAPS

OUR arrival meant a move was needed – so Dad built another lovely house for us in Green Road, Wivelsfield Green. This uprooted the family from Haywards Heath where they had lived all their lives, and was resented by them all, except Dad.

Dad was a great man. He was our hero. Lorraine and I were lucky enough to spend quite a lot of time with him, as he was older and more successful by the time we came along.

Sunday was our special day together. Dad and I would go to collect Lorraine from Chailey Heritage and we would stop off at the tobacconists in Haywards Heath on the way home. It would be the same routine every time. Dad would lift Lorraine out of the front seat and put her into her wheelchair and wheel her in to see Mr Berry. It was sweetie heaven in there, with rows of jars lined up on the shelves. "Right, which one of you has wet the bed?" Dad would ask, so the whole of the (full) shop could hear him.

It was so embarrassing, but Dad never tired of the joke.

"Karen has," Lorraine would pipe up.

"No, I haven't."

"But your mother says that one of you wet the bed."

"It was Karen."

"I haven't wet my bed."

Of course, this would produce a lot of sniggering and laughing in the shop.

"Well, only children who don't wet the bed get sweets," Dad would continue, winking at Mr Berry behind the counter.

"That's right, girls," colluded Mr Berry.

We would keep this up for a while as we would have done anything to get our Jamboree bag. Lorraine would always try to drop me in it.

Eventually, we would get back in the car, us clutching our sweets and Dad cradling his pack of Old Holborn.

Dad also built me a treehouse in the old oak tree. It was a magical place to escape to, with the view from the little windows giving a completely different viewpoint on our house and the area.

One day, when Lorraine was home, she said to Dad: "I want to have my Sunday dinner up in the treehouse like Karen."

"No, you can't," said Mum, crossly serving up the roast. "How on earth do you think you're going to get up there, anyway, with no arms and legs? How ridiculous!"

But Dad said, "Who says she can't get up there!"

And so he undid Lorraine's belt on the wheelchair and he put her over his shoulder, like you would carry a hod of bricks and he climbed up the steep treehouse ladder. I could not see how he was going to manage really as she was wriggling and crying with laughter. He kept saying to her, "Keep still, otherwise I'll drop you!"

Once Lorraine was there, deposited on the carpet, I climbed up to join her and then Dad brought up two plates of Sunday dinner. "Your dinner, ladies," he said with a flourish, putting the food on the old-fashioned school desk which had its legs sawn off. Then he disappeared. He had made it happen – what a champion. We nearly wet ourselves laughing so much. And the funniest part? Well, that Dad had gone against our mother and she was fuming.

I can see that we caused many arguments between them, but she was just so frightening and unpleasant to us that seeing Dad defy her was so enjoyable. He was our saviour in many ways, such as not making me wear a dress when my mother insisted I should. I was such a tomboy.

When we were left on our own with our mother we were at her mercy. Being told off for being naughty or cheeky and then being smacked or slapped followed a certain ritual. She would point at us, jabbing her finger right up in our faces, telling us off in this horrid tone of voice. She would get down on the floor in front of Lorraine and wag her finger inches from her face. Lorraine would always flinch and her eyelashes would be going like the clappers because she thought Mum was going to hit her face. It was so terrifying to watch Mum being aggressive towards Lorraine. I was Lorraine's protector and would do everything in my power to help her. I would try to interfere, repeatedly pushing Mum's hand away from Lorraine's face, "Mummy, please don't hit, Lorraine; please don't hit her." I would get a smack for that, but I was so protective of Lorraine. If we had been bickering, like normal sisters, she would say: "If you don't stop this I'll bang your heads together," and we totally believed her. We were petrified of her. Lorraine used to say, "You'll get bollocked by Mum for doing that, Karen", "You'll get killed for doing that". And she still says it today.

Mum was the Wicked Witch, and Dad was our hero – simple.

# TERRIBLE (ALMOST) TWINS

THERE was a time when I remember only seeing Lorraine on Sundays, but when she was six or seven she was allowed home some weekends and during the school holidays, which was amazing. I suppose she became less hard work for our mother, and we occupied ourselves, so generally I was less of a handful. We became inseparable as sisters: we were so similar in age (almost like twins). We would always be playing together (often on the floor so I was at her level) and also arguing like normal siblings.

If we were fighting, I never, ever hit her. I just could not bring myself to hit her, but the little bugger would head butt me, without a thought. One day, she hit me so hard that I nearly had concussion and I ran to Mum, crying, "Lorraine's beaten me up."

"You'll get another clout from me if you keep telling fibs like that. How could Lorraine beat you up?"

"Honestly, Mummy, she did head butt me – really hard," I sobbed.

But, of course, Lorraine could do lots of things which Mum did not think possible.

Mum was always derogatory about Lorraine, when she was not there. 'Oh, she can't do this and she can't do that.' But, actually, you can't say that someone cannot do something until they have tried and failed. Who says Lorraine could not do something – I certainly gave her the chance to prove herself and Lorraine always had such a positive attitude. This 'can-do' mentality was instilled in her at Chailey Heritage and she was also naturally competitive. I would be doing cartwheels and Lorraine would say, "I can do that."

"Oh, good. How?"

And she did a sort of roly-poly on the floor. "There. That's my cartwheel."

"Great," I said, happy that she would try anything.

Who would had believed, after all, that she would win swimming races? Dad built a swimming pool at every house we ever owned so that Lorraine could exercise in private, without being stared at. Going to the public baths was never an option. Lorraine would swim on her back with a rubber ring around her neck and she could quite happily shuffle on her bottom up and down the pool steps. She found a freedom of movement in the water and I would often say to her, "I bet you can't beat me in a race."

"Of course I can."

So I would be on my front and would sometimes lag behind as she sped off, keeping me in her sight and laughing as she struggled ahead. I could have easily won, but I let her win on those odd occasions and I was a good enough actress that she believed she had truly won. I did not want to rob her of hope and, besides, winning gave her confidence.

There was never any question of her not joining in our games and it always amazed our family that Lorraine was accepted into my circle of friends without a thought – she was simply one of us. Obviously, there were things that she could not do herself, such as going to the toilet or cutting up food, but Lorraine's motto was 'Never give up' – she is still famous for it.

Even though Lorraine could do most things, sometimes I became her arms and legs. On Christmas morning I would always, always help her unwrap her stocking presents before I undid mine. "Has Santa been yet, Karen?" she would whisper to me from her bed. She could not sit up on her own, so I would be her eyes.

"Yes, he has!"

I would then rush over to her bed, sit her up, unpack her stocking and put the little parcels near her mouth so she could tear the wrapping paper with her teeth. Lorraine never gave me any reason to pity her, but one incident sticks in my mind as the time when I realised that life for her was actually a struggle and that if she could change her disability, she would.

One night, when we were five and six years old, we were in our bedroom (in twin beds) when she looked over to me and said,

"Do you think if we prayed hard enough, my arms and legs might grow by morning?"

"Well, let's try, shall we?" I said, going over to her bed to sit her up.

I knelt down by her bed and we closed our eyes and put our hands together. "Dear God," I prayed, "Please hear our prayer that Lorraine's arms and legs may grow by the time the morning comes, please. Thank you very much. Amen." And Lorraine said, "Amen."

I laid her down again and I got into bed. "We must go to sleep now because if we don't our prayer won't be answered."

We completely believed that this would work, because we had always been told at school that our prayers would always be answered.

The first thing I did in the morning was to look over at Lorraine. "Have they grown?" I asked, expectantly.

"No," she replied, sadly.

"Oh. Did you close your eyes when you said the prayer?"

"Yes."

"Did you put your hands together?"

"No, silly, I can't."

"Well, that's what it is then – we didn't do it properly," I concluded. "We'll do it again tonight and I'll make sure that you can get your hands together."

The following night I ran over to Lorraine as soon as our mother had gone downstairs and sat Lorraine up again. She has got these little sort of hand things and I twisted them around, trying to force them to entwine.

"I can't do it like that," she said, exasperated.

"Just do it, Lorraine!"

Eventually, she managed to get her hands together and I said another prayer, very quickly, before they fell apart again. We had closed our eyes, bowed our heads and had our hands together. We were utterly convinced our prayers would be answered this time.

Of course, in the morning, we were disappointed again. "It's obviously all a lie, this praying to God stuff! That must be why Mum doesn't believe in God."

Lorraine agreed.

And that was the last time, for many years, that I asked God for help.

Lorraine would ask me to do other things for her – I was the one she trusted, never our mother. "Look after this Bay City Roller's tape, would you?" she would ask me. "I know you like it, but you're not to play it, just look after it. I don't want to take it back [to Chailey] because someone will pinch it."

Lorraine had no lockable cupboard to put her things in, so people would pinch things – her worldly goods were not safe. And did I ever play it? Of course not. I had promised her. I always felt that I must never betray Lorraine. Perhaps, if she had been a 'normal' sister, with arms and legs, I might have gone back on my word. But with Lorraine, it would have been unforgivable to let her down.

I was always so very sad when, on Sunday teatime, we realised we had no time left – it was the end of the weekend and time for us to be separated again. As soon as we arrived back at Chailey, all the kids were like bees round a honey pot because a lot of them did not get taken out as often as Lorraine. They would be trying to hold our mother's hand, which she hated, and would be asking us what we had been up to. And then it was time, all too soon, to leave Lorraine behind.

I can still remember the drive home without her, that sadness in the pit of my stomach. I am still thankful for the childhood we shared and the fun times we had, even for the fights, because I was then to lose that close connection to Lorraine for many decades. Thankfully, we have re-established that sisterly bond we carved out at Wivelsfield Green.

# ROUNDING THE CORNERS

## The Highlands, Cornwall, 1973

WE left Lorraine behind when we moved to Cornwall. There is no sugar-coating it. I remember being terribly upset about leaving her, and my many boyfriends, behind but I was told she would visit often and that Dad needed to get away. "You'll love it down there," they said.

It was all a big adventure. David and his then wife moved with us, as did Sue. We (Mum, Dad and myself) lived in a big mobile home on a smallholding on Blackwater Hill while Dad renovated the run-down thatched cottage on site. He was in his early 40s and already had a stress-induced stomach ulcer – he had had trouble with his business partners and he wanted to get away from 'the rat race'. It was the slower pace of life in rural Cornwall which appealed to him and he went to Cornwall one weekend, with David, and bought the farm on the spot – even my mother did not have a say. Now he was creating a beautiful house, part home for us and part B&B. And there was a swimming pool for Lorraine. We were living the dream.

Well, they might have been, but I certainly was not. I would sit for hours pining for Sussex and my best friend, Mark. In his first letter to me he enclosed a small ring with a skull on the face – I still have it today. It might have been a childish toy, but it meant the world to me while I was battling with homesickness. I would write to Mark about life in Cornwall and he would tell me news of Wivelsfield. It was all such innocent stuff. But then I noticed Mark's envelopes had been tampered with. I asked my mother.

"Oh, yes, I steamed it open."

"What…? Why?"

"Because I wanted to see what you write to each other. You're not having secrets from me," she glared at me.

But we had no secrets to tell. So, why on earth would my mother be interested? As I sat in my bedroom brooding over the unfairness of Mark's letters being monitored, I suddenly realised that when I gave my mother letters to post, she would be steaming them open before applying the stamp. I was terrified of Mum as it was and now I was seeing the escalation of the Wicked Witch in her.

Not only was my privacy being eroded, but you would have thought they would have sent me to Truro High School for Girls (they could afford to), but, no, I was sent to the local primary school.

You can see from my first school report at Blackwater, when I was 10, that times in Cornwall were tough to begin with. I arrived mid-year and had 'quite some difficulty in settling'. That was because I was not welcomed. There were only girls living on the neighbouring farms and, other than Lorraine, I had never played with girls before – I had only played with boys. I did not know how to relate to these harsh, pony-owning, farm girls. They were much more rough and tumble than Sussex girls and were actually more like boys, but I was still terrified of them and would try to stay out of their way in the fight-filled playground, but how I stood out. I was 'The Frog' (foreigner) and I was viewed as posh because of my accent. It was not just that I had a southern accent, but that I used the Queen's English, with the added poshness acquired through elocution lessons.

Lorraine and I had had these lessons at home on Sunday mornings when were in Wivelsfield Green. They were not really for my benefit, but I did them anyway to keep Lorraine company. She had damaged her teeth so often, by falling over, that her speech was impaired. Her little flapper hands were completely useless when it came to breaking a fall and when she toppled over on her artificial legs, or tumbled out of her wheelchair, she would smash her face on whatever surface she happened to be on and her teeth were always being repaired. So, the lovely Mrs Wells would arrive and we would have to say all these tongue twisters and speech exercises to overcome Lorraine's impediment.

Set against the Cornish dialect, my accent caused great hilarity and I was teased mercilessly. On top of that, I also started my periods. I had absolutely no idea why I suddenly started to bleed and I honestly thought I was going to die. I eventually told Sue that I was soon for The Afterlife, and she explained periods to me. And on top of that, when Lorraine did come down to stay for six weeks in the Summer holidays, the girls would call her 'spastic'. If I had not been so scared of them, I would have knocked them out for saying that.

In the end, I got accepted (rather uneasily) into the Blackwater gang because I surrounded myself with animals; the real icebreaker was my pony called Trigger and a donkey called Candy, who had a foal called Floss. Dad bought them for me – he realised they would be the key to my integration.

When I was 11, I went to Tolgus County Secondary School, where, again, I was unsettled as I had to find another new group of friends. God, it was such a rough place. There were always vicious fights in the playground and I had never seen anything like it. It was like fairy cakes in Sussex, compared with this school in Redruth. I was absolutely shit-scared most of the time and I was continually being taken to the doctors with tummy ache, because I did not want to go to school.

The only thing that was good about school was that, bizarrely, Dad wrote to the school telling them to stop setting me homework as it was eating into the time I had to help him and do chores. "You have her for six hours a day," he wrote to the headmaster, "you shouldn't be so incompetent that she needs to work at home." Dad did not really agree with formal education anyway and he thought that one could drift along quite happy at school.

The other pupils were jealous of my not doing homework, and I was more than happy not to. I do think now that this avoidance of extra work did not really help my education. Before leaving Sussex, I had to have help with my reading because I was a 'slow reader' and had been put into a special group, so I was already getting behind before I went to Cornwall. Oddly, down there, they thought I was at the appropriate reading level so when we eventually moved back to Sussex, I was really struggling with my English lessons. Could I have been dyslexic in primary school? There were certainly the early signs as my English reports comment on my work suffering from 'her casual attitude towards it. Unfortunately, she needs constant supervision in class to ensure a finished piece of work.'

For Dad it was my practical and entrepreneurial skills which needed encouraging. "Right," he said one morning, "we're going to have chickens. We're going to build some runs and houses and we're going to sell the eggs at the end of the lane and you're going to pick up the eggs every day." So, that is what he and I did. We worked together as a team and pretty soon we had chickens running about the place.

His next step was to say, "Right, that field there, you can have it for yourself and make of it what you will." It did not take me long to decide what I wanted to do. I got the lawnmower out, which was much taller than I was, and copying Dad I put my foot on the wing and pulled hard on the handle to get the mower to start. But it was so bloody hard. I kept trying and trying until I eventually started it. Just peeping over the top of the handlebar, I managed to mow half of the field and then I got a piece of wood and painted on it: 'Camping. 50p a night.' I put the sign at the top of the lane, put up some tents, cleaned out the toilet in the outhouse and put some toilet paper in there, made sure the outside tap was working and provided some buckets. And – bingo – the holiday makers started to come. I would show them around my camping facilities and they would say, "Ah, but there's a campsite up the road that's got showers."

I would reply, "Yes, but that costs £1 a night."

I was a right little businessman; I got a lot of takers by undercutting the professionals.

I can remember people coming to the house, wanting to pay, and my Dad calling for me. It was my business, so I collected the money and many guests were genuinely shocked by this little tot running the show. Before the camping season, I would also make money selling the daffodils which used to pop up in the field. I would sell them at the top of the lane for 3p a bunch.

Apart from the entrepreneurial spirit which awoke in me, Cornwall also began to mould my spirit. A turning point for me was Pedro dying. He was one of my donkeys and he was ill. The vet had been to see him and told us he probably would not last the night so I went out to the barn and cuddled up amongst the straw, with Pedro's head on my lap.

I felt so sorry for him. I had been riding him that day, out with the local girls who were all on their ponies, and he had had trouble keeping up with them. "Come on, Pedro," they kept shouting. In the end, one of the girls jumped off her pony, picked a sprig of holly from a bush and I turned around to see her sticking it under Pedro's tail. Then she gave his dock [the top part of the tail] a great whack with her hand and I nearly fell off as Pedro leapt forward. He certainly sped up then, but it knackered him out. And that is why he was dying. Pedro and I were both, in our own ways, at the mercy of those girls.

My mother came in to the stable and told me to get to bed. "But, I'm sleeping here with Pedro. I'm not letting him die on his own. I'm not doing it."

"You'll come to bed and do as you're told," Mum argued.

"I'm not." This was the beginning of me answering back. I was still scared of Mum, but I was so passionate that night – Pedro was not going to die alone.

In the end, Dad overrode my mother and he came out to the barn every now and then to make sure I was alright, and I slept the night with my dying donkey.

I woke the next morning with Pedro dead in my arms. Dad was brilliant as he made me a wooden casket with brass handles and, supposedly, Pedro's ashes were inside. I knew by then that we would be moving back to Sussex so I did not want to bury him in Cornwall. He lived in my bedroom, safely on the shelf. After the holidays we had a 'What did you do in the Summer' discussion in class and when it was my turn I told them, with tears in my eyes, about Pedro. I ended with the flourish, "And he died in my arms," and the whole class absolutely pissed themselves laughing. I had the corners knocked off my emotions that night and day. I toughened up and eventually I learnt how to fend off the bullies.

The Cornwall experience instilled the substance in me and I started to get my voice. And, although it disturbed my formal education, the time I spent with Dad made me the entrepreneur I am today. I also started to believe in God again, after several years of not believing in him – well, he never answered Lorraine's prayer for limbs. He did, however, return Tabby. He was our cat and he disappeared for weeks, and weeks, and weeks. I was distraught, but my mother kept saying, "Oh, for goodness sake, Karen. Grow up and get over it." I just could not stop crying, thinking of him on his own out in the Cornish wilds, and I prayed every night to God. Then, after seven weeks, who should appear half dead, with a septic rat bite on his face? Tabby died soon afterwards, but he had come home and that made me so happy. It was a miracle. There is a God after all.

# RETURN OF THE NATIVE

I found our next house in a Sussex property newspaper which we had delivered. Baldings Farm was a part-renovated, two-bedroom cottage and it was back in Wivelsfield Green. "That's my house, that," I said, pointing it out to Dad. "You must go and see it." I thought, wrongly as it turned out, that returning to our Sussex patch would be wonderful. I would slip back into my old life, with my little boyfriends, and we would be able to see Lorraine more often. I was so excited when Dad eventually got the bridging loan to buy Baldings and we packed up our beautiful Cornish home (then gracing the property pages of *Country Life*) and moved to Slugwash Lane.

When I put Pedro on the shelf in my new bedroom, I thought of showing Mark, my best friend in the village. This would really freak him out, I thought. But when I went to call on him, he was not at home anymore. He was now a boarder at private school. That flummoxed me. I did not understand why on earth he would leave home, aged 12. So, I tried to catch up with my other friends, but everything had changed. Boys and girls did not seem to just play together any more. With puberty approaching the boys saw me in a different light and it was too awkward to carry on our innocent friendships. I had never bothered to play with girls when I last lived in the village, so now I had no friends at all. I was even beginning to miss the Blackwater gang.

To add to my sadness, my mother then told me the awful truth about Pedro's ashes. They were in fact, she told me with obvious delight, 'off the bonfire'. I threw 'Pedro' away.

Aged 13, and in the middle of the school year, I arrived at Chailey County Secondary School (now Chailey School). Without friends, and with my now tough Cornwall-instilled exterior, I obviously had a huge hill to climb to settle in. I was also behind in my work, having been in Cornwall, and I remember finding the lessons hard. My undiagnosed dyslexia made life even more difficult for me. My first school report, July 1975, says, 'we are giving Karen the benefit of the doubt as she started very late in the year', but there were already remarks about needing to 'improve [my] attitude to work, especially in Maths' and my English spelling and grammar being 'poor', while being behind in music and lacking 'the confidence to have a go'. It was obvious Cornwall had been no good for my education.

Plus, the poor attitude. Was I just being a typical difficult teenager, or was my undiagnosed bipolar starting to raise its head? My parents thought I was just being difficult. Even Dad.

Matters were not helped when I became friends with Tara after a few weeks at the school. She was not good news, according to Mum and Dad. She had come from an approved school, was from a 'broken home' (as divorced parents were then known), lived with her social worker in our village and she was poor. Everything was against her. Yet when she faced up to me in the corridor, starting on about something, she met her match in me. I whacked her in the face and she just fell to the floor. I put my foot on her chest and said, "Don't ever do that to me again. Who the hell do you think you are?" I had obviously seen this done in the Redruth playground and instinct kicked in – no one was going to push me around. I walked away, leaving her still in a heap.

A couple of days later she came up to me and shook my hand. "I want to be friends," she said. Fine. Me and her, we were nicknamed 'The Lads'. Nobody would come near us. I had never had a best girlfriend before and we were inseparable; she was completely fascinating to me and we were so powerful together. It was a fantastic feeling as the tables had turned – I was no longer the one being bullied and if Tara was the instigator of a fight then I followed along like a little lost lamb.

My mother certainly did not want me mixing with this 'dark' person and she forbade me to see Tara out of school. She was a 'jailbird' because she had been to 'prison' (the approved school) and she wore make up and looked a bit rough. Of course, I would just sneak out of the house to visit her. I was a rebel now. It was intoxicating having a friend like her.

Looking back, we must have been so frightening and we were the school bullies – something I am not proud of today. Only recently, I joined a local sports club and this lady recognised me and made a beeline to talk to me: "Are you Karen Braysher?"

"Yes," I said, pleasantly.

"Well, you made my sister's life hell at school."

I could have died. I wondered how many more people I needed to apologise to.

Tara was a bad influence on me – that is for sure – and, for once, my mother was probably right. Tara had no conscience, whereas I did. I had a good heart buried beneath the hard exterior, but I needed this friendship so desperately.

My parents, on the other hand, were equally desperate for me to not get involved in trouble and they began to discipline me. They started their campaign in the Summer holidays, when no one could see the physical evidence.

# A LOADED GUN

WHEN I say my parents disciplined me, what I really mean is that my father was the bullet in my mother's gun. I blame her totally for what started to happen and I totally blame her for ruining my relationship with Dad. She was always jealous of our closeness and now she had the ammunition she needed to unleash revenge. Cold and calculated revenge. She was probably going through The Change, and my hormones were kicking in, and there was Dad – the only male in the house and one who was wound up with work and by a daughter who seemed to be turning into a difficult teenager.

I was 14 years old. Living in a lovely house, down a rural lane, where no one could hear me screaming.

The first time it happened, it was cold and wet – a typical Summer you may say – and we were about to go down to Cornwall for a holiday. I was in the dining room with my mother, sorting through a pile of washing to take with us, when I knocked my glass over, spilling orange juice on to the carpet. Gulp.

"Oh dear, I've spilt my juice. I'll get something to clean it up," I said, moving towards the kitchen.

"You've done that on purpose," spat my mother.

"No, I haven't. It was an accident."

She pushed passed me. "I'm going to find your father."

This had started to happen recently. Mum would find a small thing I had done wrong and run to Dad, usually in tears. Perhaps it was because of my bad school reports, perhaps he was stressed with work, perhaps he and Mum had been arguing already, but it was my mother's gunpowder which lit his undiagnosed bipolar fuse. I knew Dad would be angry was hell.

I had never really seen this anger before, but Sue and David always knew to get out of his way when he was provoked. I had seen Dad throw things in rage, but had never been scared of him.

But now I was petrified because I heard him roar. I ran upstairs, ducked as I entered my bedroom (because of the low beam) and locked the door. I hoped this, plus my weight leaning against the old door, would keep the fury away from me.

I heard him thud, thud, thud, coming up the stairs. Do you know, I had already wet myself.

"Unlock the door," he thundered, and started kicking at the timber. I knew it would not hold for long.

I put on my strongest voice: "No, I'm not unlocking the door. I don't want to."

I could feel him pushing harder. "We do not have locks in this house," he shouted and with that, the door came tumbling down. He had kicked it in.

The thing which terrified me the most (during this first time and in subsequent beatings) was that he looked completely possessed – like a frightening monster. He was gritting his teeth, his face was red and he looked enraged. He seemed to be bigger than he actually was.

He grabbed hold of me by the hair and he carried me down the stairs, lifting me off my feet. Handfuls of my hair fell to the floor as he then threw me down onto the cold bricks of the kitchen floor. It was unbelievable. The whole episode was so quick. The sequence of events was utterly stunning. There was no court; there was no jury; there was no fairness in this. I was just accused and found guilty.

His punishment was to kick my head in. Quite literally. "You will not spill things deliberately." Smash. "You will behave." Smash. His boot connected to my head again, and again. Smash. Smash. Smash. This was uncontrolled rage. He then concentrated on my shoulders and chest, kicking them with such force. I think this first real beating was such a shock that all I could do was try and protect myself from his blows.

Somehow I managed to escape and I ran out of the house, with just socks on, and I ran and ran like I had never run before. I hid behind the war memorial, of all things, in the village because it was the only place I could take shelter. I knew they would come looking for me and as I strained to listen, I could hear the sound of the car being ferociously revved up. They came roaring up the road, and I crouched down as they passed by. I knew where they were going. Up to Tara's house. But I was not stupid enough to go there. So, I went along the hedge and walked across the field and cut across another. I must have been in shock because this was unbelievable – Dad had beaten me up. I was urine-soaked and bloodied when I eventually came to the council houses at the top of the village, where I knew Tara's friends lived. I just hoped they were in.

Barry was an antiques dealer and a retired boxer, and I could think of no other place to go. As the door opened, I brushed past him, "Let me in. Let me in," I said. "My Dad's just beaten me up. I can't go home. You've got to look after me."

Poor Barry. What a shock for him.

"But your dad will come looking for you," he said.

"Yes, I know. You'll have to hide me." I knew he would protect me.

His girlfriend appeared in the kitchen, wondering what the commotion was, and took one look at me. "Let's get you tidied up, shall we?"

As I was being cleaned and changed, Barry called to me, "We've got to find a place for you to hide."

The house had a pantry and, astonishingly, in the pantry was this huge metal bread bin. It was one that sat on the floor and Barry, being an antiques dealer, must have picked it up from a hotel clearance.

"Can you get in there?" he asked as I came back into the kitchen, still shaken and feeling extremely cold.

I looked at the bin he was pointing to.

"Well, if I have to, I will. But can you find Tara for me? I'd like her to be here."

Barry sent one of his sons off to find my best friend.

When she arrived, Tara was shocked at the state I was in. She hugged me so tightly it hurt and I just released my tears. I felt safe for the first time since the beating.

"I think you should stay the night here, Karen. You can sleep on the sofa and we'll take you to see a social worker first thing," Barry said, after I had stopped sobbing. I did not have any idea what the social worker would be able to do, but I was glad someone would help me.

Later that afternoon… Knock, Knock.

We all knew who it was.

Tara and I curled up together on the sofa, and Barry went to answer the door.

"Is my daughter here?" asked my dad.

"No, she was here, but she's gone. Do you enjoy hitting your little girl?" Barry asked. "She had a split lip, black eyes and God knows what. Did you enjoy doing that?"

I could hear my father trying to speak again, but Barry drowned him out. "But she's not here now," was the last I heard, before Barry shut the door in my dad's face.

Barry came back into the sitting room. "I bet the Police will be round next. You'd better get in that hiding place." About ten minutes later, there was another knock at the door. "We want to search the property, Sir. We have reason to believe you have kidnapped Karen Braysher," said the policeman.

"Well, come in, officer. Have a look round. She was here, as I told her father, but we sent her back home. These things happen in families. Yes, have a look in the pantry. Have a look. Come in."

Well, of course, I had got inside the bread bin. We had practised it and once I had contorted my limbs and managed to squeeze in, Tara (who had been hissing, "Quickly, get in, get in!") had put the lid on top and I sat there quiet as a mouse. I can remember sweating and nearly wetting myself when I heard the policeman come into the room. They searched the whole property, but never looked in that bread bin – but then, you would never think a person could hide in one?!

Tara stayed with me after we drew all the curtains and had something to eat. Barry gave me a cuddle. "Don't worry. We're going to take you somewhere in the morning. Your dad will never do this to you again."

They were good to their word and we went to the Child Guidance Clinic in Lewes to meet a social worker. "I'm not leaving this child," announced Barry, "unless you promise not to take her home. That man is not suitable to be a father. Look at the state of her." The social worker promised. There was talk of my going into Colward, an annexe of St Francis Hospital, for children and adolescents with mental illnesses, but there was no reason to admit me.

"What would you like to happen?" the social worker asked me. I was suddenly very cold again, even though it was the Summer, and all I could manage to say was, "I don't know, but I don't want my dad to ever hit me like that again." I made her promise to never tell them where I had stayed. "I'll only go back if you agree to say that I slept in a barn for the night." There was no way I was going to get the man who had saved my life, and my sanity, into trouble. He was the best.

I cannot remember the reception when I got home, but still to this day Mum believes I slept in a barn. She tried to give me a cuddle, but I pushed her away. She persisted and in the end I started to cry. It absolutely broke my heart to think that Dad had given me that beating. It was so shocking and heart-breaking that somebody I loved could do that to me. I turned into a lost little soul. And then here she was, the gunpowder, comforting me. "You know that this is all for your own good. We've got to teach you to behave."

But, after that beating, they came regularly and I began to match Dad with my spirit and I fought against him. I would put my hands over my head and I would shout back: "You can hit me all you like, but you'll never break me." This obviously made him more mad, but my unbreakable voice came from somewhere. Was it my bipolar replying to his?

During an attack, after what seemed an eternity, I would hear my mother's voice saying, "That's enough, Reg. Stop it. Stop that now. You mustn't hit her any more. That's enough now." And the beating would stop. It was almost like he would come to, and realise what he had done. But there was never an apology. He would just walk out, leaving me with split lips, black eyes, bumps on my head and bruising all over my body. I even had welts, because of the force he used. There was no holding back.

The worst part was that she would stand there and allow it to happen. I hated her and I blamed her. My dad had excuses – perhaps he was mentally ill and he was also under a lot of pressure: from Mum, from work, from looking after his elderly mother and dealing with a stroppy teenager. He was a ticking bomb. She was my mother, the one who should have protected me.

At the time, I was utterly convinced that my real mother would one day come for me. It was a way of coping with the abuse, I suppose. "You can't be my real mother when you treat me like that," I would tell her regularly. She would just either ignore me, tut or try to cuddle me. One day, after a beating, she decided to end this fantasy I had. "I've found your birth certificate," she said, handing me the evidence I simply could not, and did not want to, believe in. "There," she pointed. I read in disbelief:

MOTHER: Brenda Phyllis Braysher
OCCUPATION: House Wife

I was absolutely gutted.

She denies that the beatings were that bad, even now. Yet how could I remember so many little details? I can only write about this beating, and the many subsequent ones, because I had counselling. But I will go to my grave remembering the abuse. It is imprinted on my mind.

Unfortunately, the only one who ever witnessed a beating was a friend called Tracey, who was staying with us for a few days. She burst into tears when Dad had me on the floor and declared we were all mad, before running upstairs to collect her things and fleeing the house. I caught up with her in the lane and pleaded with her to come back, but she was terrified and went to stay with another friend in the village.

There was only one other person who knew about the early beatings and that was my sister, Sue, but I knew not to go to her again. I had managed to escape once from a beating and in desperation I ran out of the house, again with no shoes on, and went across the fields up to Haywards Heath. I was going to see Auntie Gill and I knew vaguely where she was. I did eventually find her bungalow and I knew she would believe me – it would be easy to see that I had been beaten because I was, again, dripping with blood.

However, I stood outside her front door and with my finger

centimetres from the doorbell I had a thought: She will believe me, but if I tell her then she'll get into trouble with Mum for interfering. I already knew that Mum and Dad had stopped her, and other aunts, seeing Lorraine while we were in Cornwall and there had been huge arguments about access to Lorraine, ending in solicitors' letters barring them from taking her home at weekends. I did not want to drag her into more conflict. In the end, I talked myself out of knocking on that door to a safe haven. Instead, I walked back and went to my sister's house and knocked. "Where have you been?" she demanded. "Mum and Dad are going mad looking for you."

"But they've beaten me up. I had to run away. Look at me," I said. I looked a complete mess, yet all she could say was, "Yes, so what. You probably deserved it."

She went to the telephone and called them to come and collect me. I never, ever, ever trusted her again. I should have rung Auntie Gill's bell, but I was afraid for her.

"GET IN!" I was told when their car arrived and I was driven home. I knew what would come next, because it always did. Mum would come into my bedroom and give me a cuddle and say, "Now, you know that it's for your own good." For my own good?

Those beatings would happen so regularly, every week or so, but always in the holidays or the start of the weekend so that the injuries would heal. I came to believe that being beaten by your parents was part of everyone's childhood. It was a normal thing, in my eyes. I used to think it was my fault that they beat me, because I was getting bad school reports, hanging out with Tara and being generally obnoxious. They were telling me it was for my own good, so I had no reason to disbelieve them.

Despite this, I must have had an inkling that what was happening to me was not right because I remember going to church (which made me emotional anyway) with my parents for a christening and I spent the whole day randomly crying, and trying to hide it. It was so embarrassing and Mum would look down at me as if I was a piece of dirt and mutter at me, out of the corner of her mouth, "Stop it. Pull yourself together." She was so very dominating and secretly mean, yet putting on her airs and graces in front of everyone; the veneer of respectability.

# MUSICAL ESCAPE

TARA was my only friend, and then she got taken away from me – or rather she was expelled before the Christmas holidays in 1975. I kept in contact with her through letters, but I knew they were being tampered with by my mother (as she had done with Mark's letters). I was now on my own.

I had lost my best friend and I was at a loose end. Many of the children at school were still scared of me and I think I, in turn, was probably feeling a bit vulnerable. I was certainly bereft without Tara. I missed her tremendously. However, my school work did improve, which pleased everyone, not least my parents.

But without Tara, I went on to find another distraction. Or rather, music found me. I was just looking for somewhere warm to be, rather than standing in the cold playground at break.

It had been snowing and I wondered what was going on in one of the pre-fabs, so I jumped up and down to see through the windows. I caught a glimpse of a gas fire in the room. I also saw three boys sitting in front of a teacher and they were playing guitars. Oh, that's a nice way to get warm, I thought to myself.

"I'm going in there," I announced to the two girls I was with, "I'm going to ask if I can do that."

"But you won't be allowed to. It's a boy's thing. Girls don't play the guitar. Don't be silly."

But I had no qualms. I was going in.

"Please, Sir, can a girl do this?" I asked as I went into the warm room.

I stood there warming my hands while the teacher said, "Well, lads, what do you think?" I recognised two of the boys as being in my class. They looked at each other and nodded, as boys do.

"What's your name?"

"Karen Braysher, Sir."

"Well, Karen, go down to the music room and bring back a guitar."

And that is how my love affair with music began.

The boys – Tim, Michael and Martin – ended up being my best friends and we would end up in a band called Silver Spray, but that was a while off because the lesson I joined was only their second one.

I went home that night, completely hooked. "I'm going to learn the guitar," I announced.

"Oh, that will be a five-minute wonder," said my mother, across the table.

But it was not. The weekly classes were not enough for me and because we could not bring the school guitars home with us, I asked my parents if I could have a guitar. Predictably, the answer was no. So, I went down the road to the council houses, where the lady who took in the local papers lived and asked if I could do the deliveries. "It's life or death," I said, almost hysterically. "I simply have to get this job. I'll die if I don't, because I have to buy a guitar." She was so taken with my story that she gave me the weekday *Evening Argos* round, and then a round on Sunday.

I say it was a matter of life and death, and in my mind it was. Playing guitar completely engrossed me. We went to Brighton to get my first guitar when I had saved enough and I sat in front of the TV on Saturday mornings watching *Learn Guitar*. There was a book to accompany the Open University series and I was so determined I was going to learn. And I absolutely did.

The boys and I became quite good and in the end we started teaching the younger children how to play in the lunch hours, because it was so cold outside, and we would be asked to play for school assemblies. I remember one day we were supposed to be playing *When I needed a neighbour, were you there, were you there?*, but, at my instigation, we ended up playing *Pinball Wizard*. I might have been gaining brownie points with my guitar playing from teachers, but I still had that naughty streak.

My school report for February 1976 showed an improvement in behaviour (probably because I was no longer so influenced by Tara), although I was still struggling at school, mainly because of unrecognised dyslexia. I was being labelled as disruptive in classes

I found too hard, because I would prefer to play up, if asked to read in class, rather than look thick. I really did believe that I was stupid and I also believed I was a bad person and that it was my fault I got beaten at home. It is not difficult to see that I had no self-confidence or self-worth and the only thing that saved me was my guitar.

On my bedroom door I had a sign made, 'Genius at work – Do not disturb'. I would spend days at a time, holed up there. "What colour are the leaves on the trees?" Dad would say to me. "You've been in there so long, it's Autumn." But then Dad encouraged my playing. It was my escape from everything and he was happy, when being good Dad, to pay for lessons and sheet music.

I was completely obsessed with music. It took over my life – it is a very bipolar thing to fixate on something. I was driven to be the best guitar player and it was something positive that could not hurt me; something that loved me back. And nobody could take it away from me.

Music also gave me a solid group of male friends and, being a tomboy at heart, this suited me beautifully. I was in my element.

# DOWNHILL GRADES

THE next step was to move to electric guitars as the boys and I could then form a proper band and we already had another boy from the village lined up to play drums. We made a pact to all ask our parents for the guitars as Christmas gifts – this was 1976.

"It's a matter of life and death," I told my parents, as I handed them my letter to Santa Claus. 'ELECTRIC GUITAR' was all I had written. But I was not sure I would get one, because of my behaviour at school.

A mix of undiagnosed dyslexia and the first stirrings of undiagnosed bipolar was never going to make school easy for me. I was rude, sullen, uncooperative, obstructive, easily distracted and ready to distract others, according to school reports.

There were some subjects I liked, such as Art and Music and Environmental Studies, but that was mainly because of the teachers. They were women (strangely, I had no respect for male teachers even though I had male friends) and they were intelligent and each had a touch of flamboyancy about them. Being bipolar, I was naturally drawn to more eccentric people (perhaps I saw myself in them) and they encouraged and inspired me, particularly Mrs Bensusan, my Music teacher. She once took me, and another girl, to see *The Messiah* at the Brighton Dome and I particularly remember having to stand during the 'Hallelujah Chorus'. When we came out of the Dome, Mrs Bensusan said, "Well, girls, shall we paint the town red?" She was such a lovely older lady. So eccentric; an artist. I was completely taken with her – she was a proper mother figure – and she continued to be my greatest advocate all the way through school.

But other teachers were too dry, too thick and too male to earn my respect.

Letters from the headmaster started to arrive at home – before and during the Summer holidays. The beatings got worse again. It is interesting to note that the symptoms of bipolar were showing at this time – the headmaster wrote in one letter: "She is very erratic and appears determined not to co-operate with some teachers and seems to believe, quite erroneously, that they treat her unfairly. She can (and has) talked quite sensibly to me about her difficulty in controlling her temper, but obviously I must insist that she behaves and talks to teachers and other pupils in a socially acceptable manner."

I was really in a difficult place. Beatings at home, with no one to turn to, undiagnosed dyslexia and bipolar at school. The only solace I had was music, and that kept the bouts of depression from becoming too much to bear. The boys and I would rotate the venue for our weekly practice to each others' houses and when it was my turn to host, my parents would have to leave for the evening. Dad was particularly supportive of the band and he would take me to Plumpton, where the boys lived, and collect me. It was Tim who gradually came forward as the band leader and he decided that I should be the lead singer, because I was the only girl. So, despite being a rubbish singer, I was forced to sing and I got used to it.

The worst punishment my mother could mete out was to ban me from going to band practice; beatings I could cope with, but the band was different. I could not, and would not, let them down. If I had been grounded, I would climb out of my bedroom window, having already lowered my guitar and music to the ground by a piece of string, and clamber onto the apple tree and get myself down to the ground. I would make no sound and run along the bottom of the garden, along the fence line, and out into the lane. It was a commando operation. I would then walk the four miles to Plumpton and rehearse. I would usually be given a lift back by someone's mum as they did not want me to walk back in the dark, but I would make them drop me at the top of the drive so I could sneak back in – I was never found out. But I was prepared to take a beating because there was no way that I would let the boys down. We were like the Musketeers and if I said I was going to be there, I would be.

I would tell the boys it was all my mother's fault – she was the stupid one, the argumentative one, the one who I hated. I never told them about the beatings because, firstly, it would have been too embarrassing, and also I wanted them to still like my dad, so nobody knew what I was going through.

When I went back to school in September 1976 – aged 14 – the school must have expected, or at least hoped for, a change in my behaviour. But they were disappointed – and so were my parents. My behaviour, speech, dress and general demeanour were appalling. Another letter home stated that if I did not keep out of trouble they would have no option but to suspend me as the list of incidents was getting out of hand. My first suspension happened in October. This was for repeatedly smoking at school and on the coach, and I had been repeated reported by Karen the Head Girl. Now, Karen was interesting. At school, she was all goody-two-shoes, bossy and pedantic and I really hated her and used to disobey her and even swear at her, but I think that was probably for appearances, because it was cool to hate the Head Girl. Outside of school, she and I played in the village stoolball team and we got on fine. I remember her saying to me, "You're not a bad person, Karen. Deep down inside you're a very good person. So, why do you do it? One minute you're aggressive, the next you're nice." And that stayed with me, because she could see how mixed up I was and basically out of control.

I was so wild, by then, that either my parents asked the school for help, or they accepted the offer of help from the school, and I came to the notice of the Area Education Officer in Lewes and, thankfully, I was assigned a social worker from the Child Guidance Service (now known as Family Consultation Centre). And that social worker, Mrs Perkins, saved me. Auntie Gill and Auntie Hazel would tell my mother that I was hyperactive on the odd occasion I went to stay with them and my cousins, but my parents were adamant there was nothing wrong with me – I was just naughty. And I believed I was naughty. It was something I could not help; I was just bad. But Auntie Gill, Auntie Hazel and Mrs Perkins had faith in me and told me that I was not a bad person.

Mrs Perkins would collect me from school regularly and we would talk in my bedroom for hours and sometimes she would talk to my parents. I had no idea what she was trying to do, but I was quite pleased to have her to talk to because I certainly did not have a friendship with my mother. I had no positive female role model and I felt lost. I do not think I told her about the beatings, although she was certainly aware of my ambivalence towards my mother. I suppose I was able to vent my feelings to Mrs Perkins, but at that point I think without medical intervention it was inevitable that I would carry on causing trouble at school. By November I was suspended again, this time, I am sad to say, for 'intimidating and kicking' some younger girls. However, Mrs Perkins did manage to get me moved to a lower English class so I was less pressured. I tried to call Mrs Perkins at her office just before Christmas to wish her happy holidays and I got a letter in reply, including the following which buoyed me up: "I and many other people have tremendous faith that things can all come right in the end! So don't give up!!"

The only thing which kept me going through those awful school suspensions was the thought that I might get the longed for electric guitar that Christmas, but the odds seemed stacked against me.

Christmas Day dawned. Lorraine and I woke up, excited.

"But there's no electric guitar," I wailed, looking at the unwrapped presents at the bottom of my bed. For the first time ever, I had opened my presents before helping Lorraine open hers. I cannot tell you how upset I was. The future of the whole band was in the balance.

I just could not believe my father had denied me a guitar – he knew how much it meant to me. After Lorraine had finished with her presents, I helped her down off the bed and we went to our parents' room.

"Perhaps it's in their room," I reasoned. "It would be too big to fit on my bed." But there was nothing in their room.

"Happy Christmas, girls," said Dad, smiling. "Are you missing something, Karen?" he added, noting my sad expression.

"Yes," I said, expectantly.

"Well, have a look over there."

I ran over to the corner which was hidden from view and there it was – my electric guitar.

Back then, you could not just text your friends to see if everyone had got a guitar. We had to wait until returning to school to find out. "Did you get one?"

"Yes."

"Did you?"

"Yes."

"So did I."

"And you, Karen?" asked Tim, looking at me hopefully.

"YES!"

We had this big group hug, full of relief that our plan had worked. And Silver Spray was born – named after a fish and chip shop in Lewes which the boys passed every Wednesday on their way to college.

Being the only girl in the band, and playing electric guitar, gave me so much status at school. I was so cool in my mates' eyes, especially when Silver Spray began to play at Plumpton Youth Club. I was totally obsessed with my music, and being in the band was the be-all and end-all. I finally had some self-confidence and self-belief in my abilities. Music was something I could do, very well – my brain worked differently when it came to playing music.

# BRUISING REVEALED

DESPITE my parents getting me the guitar, probably in the hope that I would sort myself out, my behaviour at school nose-dived after Christmas and, again, I was referred to the Child Guidance Service for 'aggressive and disruptive behaviour at school'.

It is clear from letters I have found that my parents were confused and bewildered by my behaviour and it seems they did admit that there were some violent scenes at home as a result of disagreements. I had an assessment meeting with Mrs Perkins in February 1977 and it is clear that I was suffering from bad moods, anger and upset feelings which stopped me concentrating on school work. I had trouble obeying school rules and working in class, because I did not know how to do the work (the dyslexia) and I could not be bothered. It is clear I was carrying home life, and beatings, into school with me and I had to try very hard to control the desire to shout and swear at teachers and pupils who wound me up. Mrs Perkins was trying to get me to see that people were concerned about me and trying to help me, but that my behaviour was causing people to be angry with me. I had to try and think twice before 'going off on one'.

Most telling is Mrs Perkins' remarks about how I was feeling about home: "1) parents having a changing attitude towards the school, 2) parents disagreeing about Karen, 3) being wanted in the first place and being wanted now." The arguments, hostility, beatings and the 'wish we'd never had you' speech were making me angry, sad and hurt. What a mess.

It is obvious my parents disagreed privately, and publicly, with each other and the school about what should be done with me. When it was first suggested I should be taken out of Chailey and sent to the Tutorial Unit at Newhaven they were adamant I should stay in mainstream schooling. Dad would tell me, "You're not mad, Karen, not like *One Flew Over The Cuckoo's Nest*. We don't want you sent somewhere like that – where men in white coats will take you away, drug you up and brainwash you. You're just bad, not mad." The school obviously realised I needed specialist behavioural support, which they could not provide.

Mrs Perkins was trying to establish, properly, what was going on. She was making a link between my behaviour and what was going on around me, but I could not stop my 'badness', even when I wanted to. It just leaked out – that is what bipolar does to you. It is said that bipolar usually rears its ugly head in the late teens, early 20s, but remember I started my periods aged 10, so there is the possibility that I was a little advanced.

I was becoming such a problem that Chailey were keen to get rid of me and by mid-February, 1977, two incidents occurred which gave them the final reason, and the excuse, to exclude me.

I must have been given a beating mid-week because I went into school with these big lumps on the top of the head and I was feeling sick and confused. Two of my friends noticed I was not my usual mouthy self and asked me what was wrong. I had never ever talked to anyone at school before, but I asked them, "Does your dad ever hit you?"

"Well, yes, I might get slapped," said Anna.

"But does your dad ever hit you a bit harder?" I asked again.

They both shook their heads. I had always believed that the beatings I received were normal; it was not something I had discussed with others, I just assumed.

"I've got this bruise here," I said, showing them my chest, "and I've got these lumps on top of my head. Here, feel."

After feeling them, they exchanged looks of horror. "That's not normal, Karen. Does your dad hit you around the head and chest?"

The penny dropped.

"We'll take you to see Mrs McConville," said Linda. I was still feeling nauseous and removed from reality, so I let them lead me to the Senior Mistress. They knocked on the door and ushered me in.

After she had felt the lumps, I was told to go back to my lessons. We all thought it odd that nothing more should happen. Surely she would do something? It was not until the following lesson that Mrs McConville came into my class and called for me.

"We're going to the Headmaster's office, Karen."

"Oh, but I haven't done anything wrong, Miss."

"No, it's okay. I just want you to show him the lumps and tell him what you told me about your dad hitting you."

I could not believe it when we entered the office because there stood this older, grey-suited, balding man who I recognised as Mr Gray, the Education Welfare Officer in Lewes, who I had had dealings with before.

"Can I feel your head, Karen?" he asked. I stepped forward.

He tutted and said to me, "I'm taking you home right now."

"But I don't want to go home. I've done nothing wrong and you're making me go home?!" I was frightened. It was the last place I wanted to go.

But I had no choice and I had to get in his car and he drove me back to my parents, who were waiting for me. They had obviously been told what had happened.

"Would you like a whisky?" Dad asked Mr Gray as we entered the house. I cannot remember if Mr Gray did have a drink, but my father certainly did. I was put into the dining room, while they chatted in the lounge and I overheard Mr Gray say, "If you continue to do this, she'll be taken away from you and put into care."

I was not happy about that, either. Being put into care had done Tara no good and if I stayed here there was no one to protect me. Lorraine had no idea what was going on because I never wanted to burden her as she had her own problems and was by now living in London.

It was decided that I would stay at home that day and then a uniformed policewoman was sent to the house every day, for two weeks. She made me undress in the dining room, once in the morning and once at night, to make sure I did not have any bruising. It was very odd, but that was prevention back then. The beatings stopped for those two weeks. But then I got another bruise.

It was only a few weeks later that I had double history with Mr Wall. He was a younger teacher, who played guitar in a band, so I quite liked him as we had something in common. It was the first lesson of the morning, but I wanted to go to the loo. I had started my period and I needed to go and sort myself out. "No, you should have gone to the toilet before you came in," was his response to my request. "You'll have to wait until the tea break."

That would be another hour.

"But I can't wait until then," I said. "I need to go to the toilet."

But, of course, once he had said no, he could not back track and when I repeatedly asked him, he always said no. I thought I might wear him down, but not a chance.

I was frightened to just get up and go out, even though I was desperate to, because I had already been suspended several times and I was on my final warning. He was also bigger than me.

By the time the bell rang for break I was beside myself and I grabbed my bag and ran towards the door. But Mr Wall got in my way and pushed me back against one of the work benches, hard.

"You're not going anywhere," he said to me, as all the class streamed past me.

I could see them beginning to appear at the window, looking in at what was going on between me and the teacher. He was keeping me back and he was starting to go into a kind of frenzy – his hands were shaking and he was breathing heavily.

I was concentrating on him, but could hear my classmates outside shouting, "Bundle. Bundle, Karen Braysher." I was a known troublemaker, and here I was squaring up to a male teacher. This was not the case, but that was what everyone saw. Then Mr Wall did something which I had not bargained for. There was a back room, the equipment store, at the side of the classroom and he pushed me into this little space, which was out of sight. I very nearly wet myself, too, because I was so frightened and I had blood running down the tops of my thighs. I tried to push past him, but he kept stopping me.

He stood in front of me, shaking. "I won't have disobedience in my class," he said, towering over me. "I thought you liked me, because we both play guitar." As I looked up at him, I noticed above his head that some of the boys were obviously standing on each others' shoulders to get a view into the high-arched window which provided the only natural light into the room. A face would appear, then fall away. I was feeling really trapped and scared by now, and I was desperately wanting to go to the toilet. I began to cry. I had no idea what was going to happen next and, looking back as an adult, I think it was a sexual frenzy he was in.

He acted in the most unprofessional way and he kept saying, "I thought you liked me. I'm disappointed that you don't like me."

Eventually, the bell rang for the end of break and he seemed to come to, and he walked away from the door and let me go. I had been in that room for 20 minutes with him.

I ran like a maniac to the loo. I so nearly wet myself. As I sat there, I was really quite stunned by what had happened and when I went into the next lesson everyone thought I had had a fight with Mr Wall – such was my reputation. In fact, I had been very passive and had not become aggressive at all, which, for me, was very unusual.

That incident went down in Chailey history and people to this day still believe that I was expelled for fighting with a teacher. The truth was rather different because some days after the incident I told my father that I had a terrible bruise. It was so significant that I honestly thought my skin was going to fall off.

"Who's hurt you?" he asked, when I had shown him the mark caused by Mr Wall pushing me against the bench.

"Well, no one, really. It's just that should you tell someone if you've got a really bad bruise? Should you see a doctor or something? Is my leg going to fall off?"

"I'm taking you to the Police straight away. Who did this to you?" It is rather ironic that he would beat me up, causing all sorts of bruising and cuts, yet when someone else did it to me, the Police were notified. I suspect he was more concerned that he would get the blame for this injury, if he did not report it himself.

My bruise was photographed.

I was suspended from school and so was Mr Wall, on Valentines' Day, 1977. I was 15 years old and that was the last time I stepped foot on the school grounds. Mr Gray escorted me home and arrangements were made for me to attend an approved school. Mr Wall was reinstated.

Being expelled for fighting with a teacher was a cool thing for people to imagine. I left school on a huge high note, but the reality was much sadder. I had been passive throughout the incident and I suspect the real reason I was excluded from school, in the end, was because I was beaten up by my own father, repeatedly, and Mr Wall provided Chailey with the perfect opportunity to pass me on.

# EXCLUDED

*"My feeling about Karen was that – like many adolescents – she is moved by strongly opposed forces within herself; her behaviour gives plenty of indication of her wish to challenge authority, but I found some indications also of a wish to make a success of her social and educational relationships. Karen is not mentally ill in the formal sense, but she does need continuing help with the task of resolving her internal contradictions."*

DR ROSS – CONSULTANT PSYCHIATRIST, MARCH 1977

Dr Ross concluded that Chailey should be asked to allow me back. I so wanted to return to school because I had been excluded since the Mr Wall incident and none of my friends had written to me or been to see me. Perhaps they were told to leave me alone – I was a pariah, like Tara had been. But Chailey would not re-admit me and the County Council was adamant the best place for me – behaviourally and academically – was this Tutorial Unit which my parents were dead against: *One Flew Over The Cuckoo's Nest*, and all that. The only other option was private school or home-schooling.

This news sent me into a serious depression. "I have no future," I told Mrs Perkins. "I'll probably end up in prison, because I'm such a bad person, or in a hospital, because I'm mad." There could be no hope for me.

It must have been my parents' pushiness, and Dr Ross' conclusion that I should be in mainstream schooling, which saw me offered a place at Uckfield Technical College. However, much to my surprise, lots of people wanted to take me on. They all knew I had been excluded from Chailey and thought I was a hard nut – bad news travels fast. But I was frightened. It was a larger school, I did not know anyone and it was like the Cornwall playground all over again. I was so scared after that first day, I did not return and would bunk off and go into Haywards Heath instead to see a Chailey schoolfriend who was off with glandular fever. It was not long until my mother realised, after the school phoned her about my continued absence.

Of course, I got a beating, but I was more scared of going back to Uckfield. I would say, "I'm not going."

"You are going."

"I'm not and you can't make me."

Every time they dropped me off at the bus stop to go to school, I got off at the next stop and made my way to Haywards Heath. I just refused to go.

Eventually, my parents looked at the much smaller St Georges' House in Brighton and it was agreed by the Council that I would get a taxi there and back every day. This was in May. But my father was not happy with the education there, because I did not have an Art or Music teacher – my two best subjects. They suited my brain. He continually pushed for me to return to Chailey, but my behaviour at St Georges' was not good. Undiagnosed bipolar was leaking out.

Things were not well at home, either. One date sticks in my mind – August 16 – as this was the day Elvis Presley died, and my mother behaved, in my mind, like Aldolf Hitler. I had been playing in a stoolball tournament and my parents had always said they would buy me a pair of training shoes, rather than plimsols, if I hit two sixes during a match. Well, this day, I did. I bounded home, so pleased with myself, and asked my mother for my prize. Fair's fair. But she refused and went to slap me. I put my hand up to stop her hand and she exploded, "How dare you try to hit me!"

"But I didn't," I shouted back. I was now 15 years old and full of anger myself, yet there was no way that I would have ever hit my mother. Within a flash, she ran outside to find Dad.

"Karen tried to hit me," was all I heard. Of course, Dad flew in before I could escape and had me on the kitchen floor within seconds, kicking my head in.

I had always believed that I deserved the beatings, but that particular one I remember because it was so unfair – I never did get those promised trainers – no wonder I had issues withholding my anger when I was faced with a mother like that who would instigate a beating and watch it happen without flinching, without emotion.

Back at school after the Summer holidays, at my father's insistence, I was given the opportunity to go to Technical College one day a week on a hairdressing course (more about that later) and I got to take a C.S.E in English and also started music lessons, but then I kept being abusive to teachers and refusing to go to the College.

Dated 13th October, 1977, this letter to my parents came from St Georges' headmaster:

*"...she was also abusive of myself and of my own position, which, while it does not particularly worry me on a personal level, it is, nevertheless, again symptomatic of the very reasons why an ordinary school would not be likely to tolerate her behaviour for very long...*

*I am well aware that there are various agencies putting in considerable efforts as well as yourselves and that everyone is working on Karen's behalf, although she does not seem to appreciate that that is so. One can only trust that these efforts will prove successful in the end..."*

Everyone was exasperated with me – not least myself. If I am to really understand my parents' behaviour, with hindsight, all I can say is that they just could not cope with me and the disappointment of Lorraine's disability. Was I a scapegoat? And nobody provided, or my parents stopped them providing, the correct help. Mrs Perkins was the only one who was trying to guide me back into life and I trusted her completely. But I lost Mrs Perkins when she left her job (on maternity leave) and I went into a deeper spiral. I had lost my one rock. My new social worker, a Mrs Korner, was so much older than Mrs Perkins and I felt no connection to her. However, she was spot on about my behaviour and this letter from her to my GP, dated 1 December, 1977, is the closest anyone came to describing my creeping undiagnosed bipolar (and Dad's aggression):

*"She is a troubled girl, often overwhelmed with uncontrolled anger, and destructive feelings that alarm her; she has low self-esteem, is fairly*

*inhibited and has difficulties in establishing relationships with others, and tends to be aggressive in her attitude to the outside world. Her father, at times, has similar attitudes. She is intelligent and articulate, and more anxious than she dare admit; she cannot accept authority, perhaps because of her insecure essence of her autonomy... Although at times she manifests what seems to be only extreme forms of "adolescent rebellion" the situation does fluctuate and she has periods of tension and depression, poor sleep and violent dreams. She is certainly unhappy most of the time; her one successful outlet is her participation in an amateur 'pop' group, where she displays considerable talent. She deeply resents being deprived of a normal education, as a result of her own behaviour, and has real worries about the future and her ability to take part in the working world."*

It is obvious I was nearly at rock bottom. I had lost Mrs Perkins, had no friends and could not burden Lorraine with my feelings, my parents were arguing all the time about what was right for me and I was not happy at St Georges'. In the end, my father took me out of school all together because he was so appalled at how I was being 'educated'.

1978 dawned and I was in a sorry way. I was very unhappy, stuck at home, wondering if I was 'crazy' (and going to be carted off by men in white coats), with no exams and heading for the scrap heap. I did get a job as a 'Saturday girl' in the local hairdressers but I got sacked from that when I was asked to wear my school uniform. Of course, I did not have a uniform having been expelled from school – and my mother had got rid of it – so I went in my normal clothes and was told to leave. The manager was probably right to ask me to wear school clothes because I had been turning up in rags almost. My mother never bought me new clothes – the Family Allowance went on something else, never on me. It was the first time that I realised how disheveled I looked and it was embarrassing to think that we lived in this lovely house, yet she did not keep me properly dressed. I remember the hot tears stinging my eyes as I walked out of that hair salon, totally crestfallen and angry at my mother. She really cannot be my true mother, I thought once again.

There was the odd day I enjoyed during my exclusion and that was when I had time alone with Dad. We had that week of heart-to-hearts, when my mother and Lorraine went away to the Thalidomide Trust's guest house in Jersey, and he occasionally took me to his building site for 'work experience'. On those days he was peaceful, good Dad.

"Here's your flask of tea," I would say.

"And here's your gloves," he would reply. We would swap items and set off. I used to love working with him. He would get me to mix up concrete and would let me smoke as long as I went round the corner where he could not see me. "If I don't see you, then I can't say to your mother, 'She's been smoking.'" Eventually, my building gloves were held together by pieces of Sellotape but Dad still gave them to me at the beginning of my working day. They were definitely due for the bin. Years later, I went into his shed and asked him why my gloves were still there. "I'll never get rid of those gloves," he said, smiling at me. He could become sentimental over a pair of gloves I had worn – it was obvious he did what he did to me when he was out of control.

Dad also provided me, in a roundabout way, with a different kind of peace. He was working at the Anchorhold, which was run by monks from The Society of Saint John the Evangelist in Haywards Heath. They had tried a number of bricklayers to build their arched windows, with no success until my father was approached. The head monk, Father Herbert Slade, was so pleased with Dad's craftsmanship that he invited my parents and me to tea. I will never forget that visit. The monks were so softly spoken and gentle, in complete contrast to the environment at home, which was full of pettiness, shouting and violence. I was so taken with the place's peacefulness; I just wanted to pack my bags immediately and move in. They practised yoga, contemplative prayer and meditation and I do not know if Father Slade saw the pain and turmoil in me, but before we left he gave me a handcrafted prayer mat and a piece of paper.

As we drove home, I found some solace from turning the beautiful mat over in my hands and reading the handwritten quote on the paper:

## REVELATION

*God is always being revealed and the revelation is never complete. The Spirit who leads into all truth continually proceeds both from the divine nature in terms of revelation and from the human nature in terms of reception. There is no end to the process.*

I doubt the words meant much to me at the time, but I insisted on praying daily on my prayer mat and I found some peace from my troubled mind. I would regularly ask for help from God, to keep me out of prison or the mad house. I suppose I was waiting for someone or something to take me out of the life I was living.

Dad had always been fighting for me to have better educational opportunities and since he had taken me out of St Georges', and with Chailey still unwilling to take me back, he had no option but to get a tutor in to teach me at home. Mrs Stone, who Dad had done some building work for, was an ex-teacher living in the village, and my future rested in her hands. She came every day and she would help me with my reading and writing – I was so far behind – and we would do all sorts of handicrafts, like sewing. I started to make a patchwork quilt for a very special reason (see next chapter) and we would go on day trips to places like Ditchling (for the art) and to Brighton and the Ashdown Forest.

But the main thing I will always thank her for was taking me to Lewes to meet the East Sussex Head of Music – Nancy Plummer. This lady was a Hooray-Henry type, and I had to make my case to her so I could take the C.S.E Music exam. She looked down her nose at me as I gave my speech about being excluded from school, yet wishing to take the exam because music was my passion.

"Well," she said, "I don't see how you can take the exam, because you haven't done the required coursework. How could you pass it?"

"Well, Miss, I've done some of it and I'm sure I can catch up with what I've missed."

"There's no way to catch up, Karen." This was her final decision.

Something in me just snapped. "I'll meet you on the dole queue, then," I shouted.

"Now, now, Karen, that's no way to behave," said Mrs Stone. But I was absolutely incensed. I was being denied the one chance I had to get an exam qualification to my name, in a subject I adored.

"You can fuck off!" I shouted at Mrs Plummer, "You're all the fucking same."

In the car on the way home, in stony silence, I reflected on my behaviour. "Fuck it, I've totally blown it now," I said to Mrs Stone. She nodded in agreement. However, in the time it had taken for us to get back home – about 15 minutes – Mrs Plummer had phoned my mother and said, "I'm arranging for Karen to have private lessons. Your daughter shows amazing spirit and I have no doubt that she will pass the music exam."

"Huh?" I said, exchanging looks with Mrs Stone. "You're joking, Mum?" But she was not. I was to have lessons with Mrs Anne Ladd, twice a week, for three hours at a time. My anger vanished. If I had not gone off on one, Mrs Plummer would never have given me the opportunity – I learnt a lot that day about the importance of being passionate. And I had found an ally, Mrs Plummer, who was powerful and strong and could get things done for me.

With Mrs Stone helping me order musical scores in the library (I had never even taken out a library book before), studying compositions by Mozart, Elgar and Bach with Mrs Ladd, and my classical guitar lessons with Paul Gregory, I felt ready for the Music exam. But I was not allowed to take the exam at Chailey – I was still unwelcome – so I had to sit in a room on my own at the County Council offices in Lewes. I felt like a criminal; all alone. I had to sit three papers and each time I sat there thinking that I must be bad and/or mad to be treated in this way.

In the end, I left education at 16, with one qualification – Music, Grade Four. It was a pass. I was not happy with this, because I knew if I had been at school then I would have got Grade One, and would have passed in other subjects, too. I knew I was not stupid. However, I was glad to get the Music because I had to prove to Mrs Plummer she was right to have given me a chance. There was nothing on earth that would have stopped me passing it because otherwise I would have failed her. She gave me my opportunity and I ran with it. Maybe my prayers were being answered.

# THE LOVE OF MY LIFE

MUSIC became even more of an obsession after I finished education. It was the only thing which I had left, apart from the other love of my life – Adrian.

I had met him on Saturday, 4th June, 1977 – the Queen's Silver Jubilee. The band I was in – Silver Spray – were asked to play on the float carrying the Beauty Queen at the Plumpton and East Chilton Parishes carnival. I had my 'Purdy' haircut, wore trousers and had my sunglasses on. I was never worried about my appearance. All I cared about was playing my guitars. Following the parade there was a dance and BBQ at the racecourse and this guy came up to me and said, "How old are you?"

"Nearly 15. How old are you?"

"17."

And that was where we started. We exchanged phone numbers, although I would never have been allowed to call him on our home phone as it was too expensive and only used in emergencies. He had a motorbike, so would come over to the house on that. My mother did not like this. Neither did she like the fact that Adrian's mother was in St Francis (the mental hospital they refused to send me to) after suffering a nervous breakdown following the death of Adrian's brother who was knocked over in the road. My mother had no compassion; just saw her as a nut case.

"You know that madness runs in families," she told me, "it's catching. And if you have children with Adrian they'll be mad, too."

Dad, meanwhile, quite liked Adrian, but would carry out my mother's dirty work: "I've come out here," he would say, approaching Adrian in the drive, "because I've been told to tell you that you're not to come here with that bike, and I've also been told to tell you that Karen's not to go on the back of it. But, it does look like a very nice bike," he would add, with a wink.

At some point I was forbidden to see Adrian, which was probably because my behaviour at Chailey was getting completely out of control. But much like me meeting up with my old friend, Tara, in secret, I managed to smuggle notes to Adrian's sister and he and I would meet in The Royal Oak car park on Jacob's Corner at Wivelsfield Green up to five times a week. He knew everything about what was going on at home (especially the beating over the trainers) and it made him so angry, but he did not want to challenge my dad. His answer: "We'll have to get married when you're 16, because it's the only way to get you away from them."

"Yeah, but where will we live?"

"We'll have to get one of those new flats over the Co-op in Haywards Heath."

"But how are we going to do that? We've got no money."

"Well, I'm working." He was working as a surveyor, building the tunnel at Lewes.

The daydreaming would continue. "Do you want to have any children?" he asked.

That was easy to answer. "Yes! I want ten."

"That's quite a lot. Really? You want ten?"

Of course, I was so lonely at the time that I just wanted to be surrounded by a big family – it sounded such fun. All of Adrian's plans sounded good to me. I really did love him, and not just because he was going to provide me with an escape plan. My parents thought Adrian was not good enough for me, but I knew he was perfect. We even got matching permed hairstyles, done by my sister. It was just so funny to think back to us sitting in the private bar of the Cock Inn at Wivelsfield, with matching perms, me with my orange juice and big, butch, leather-clad Adrian, with his pint of beer.

With Mrs Perkins, my social worker, gone, it was Adrian who became my rock and he was there throughout my trials at St Georges' and I began to make a patchwork quilt with Mrs Stone, my home tutor, for our marriage bed.

"If they don't let us get married, then we'll just run away to Gretna Green. There's no doubt about it," he promised me. He was quite firm about it and would visit me at the chemist shop I worked in after I passed my Music CSE. Adrian was my world and even my music became slightly sidelined.

I meant so much to Adrian that one day, rather extraordinarily, his mother came into the chemist clutching a yellow chrysanthemum plant. She had obviously been let out of St Francis for a couple of hours and she came to see me – drugged up to the eyeballs. She was such a sad sight, shuffling in a straight line up to me, but she plonked the plant on the counter and then out came her speech: "This is a token of Adrian's love for you." And that was it. She turned around and shuffled back out the door. I have to say that I thought more of that yellow chrysanthemum than any of the red roses and wonderful bouquets I later received. That plant still stays in my mind as one of the most poignant things I have ever been bought. She was clearly trying to tell me that she liked me. It was her way of telling me and it was clearly an enormous task for someone mentally ill, and drugged, to do. I was absolutely gobsmacked by that gesture.

Things were all looking great for Adrian and me. But I just could not run away, in the end. I was too worried about where we were going to live and what we were going to do. But I should have run away with him. It would have been the making of me. But I did not. And then my mother got in the way.

Adrian and I never had sex, because I was too scared to. My mother had always drummed it in to me, "If you come home pregnant, you're out. You must not have sex." So, she was completely shocked when I told her, over a piece of cake at the local tea shop, that I was going on The Pill.

"No, you are not."

"Yes, I am."

"No, you're not. Not without my say so," she hissed, "And, anyway, if you take The Pill you will get enormously fat and you'll grow hairs on your chest."

"Don't be so ridiculous," I replied.

"You will. It's a proven fact." I began to wonder. Then she continued, "Of course, you're not going to go out with HIM anymore."

"I am. Adrian's asked me to marry him." Well, that was the end of it. She took me straight home and stood over me while making me write a 'Dear John' letter. I really did not know what

I was writing, but I believed she was right. After repeating herself several times, I believed her that I should not go on The Pill, that I was too young, that I would grow hairs on my chest and get fat. "You're better off without him, Karen. He's no good for you. He's a waster. His mother's a nutter and you'll end up a nutter or your children will. You're not going near him again."

She coerced me into writing that letter and she stood over me as I signed it. There was no need for her to steam open THAT letter, as she knew every word I had written. I sadly put my badly-spelt letter in an envelope and was going to put it in the post box, but she said, "Oh, no you don't. We're going to hand deliver it. Get in the car." She drove me to Adrian's house in Plumpton and watched me put it through the letterbox. I have to say I was still frightened of my mother at that time because she was still bigger than me and I had been pushed around so much that I just obeyed her – it was easier.

As soon as I posted the letter, I began to realise what she had made me do – dump the only person who cared about me, and the only person I cared for. I was so angry and as soon as I could I ran to the phone box.

"Is Adrian there?" I asked his sister, who picked up the phone. "No. He was here, but he's not here now," and she put the phone down. I tried several times, but when I finally got to speak to Adrian he put the phone down on me as I tried to explain that my mother had made me write the letter.

"I never wrote that letter, Adrian. It was her that wrote it and I did not have the power to stand up for myself." But my words were not heard.

I was so sad. I even turned up at a football match a month or so later as I knew he would be playing, but he was so cold to me when I finally got to talk to him in the bar after the match.

"I've got other responsibilities now," he said, meaning he had already got another girlfriend. And my mother delighted in showing me a cutting from the local paper of his marriage a few years later: "See, he never really loved you," she said, as though she had saved me from a relationship disaster.

I completely blamed my mother for that heartbreak, and I still do today – what could have been hurts me the most. I could have been so happy with Adrian, and our ten children, and I still rue the day that I did not just run away with him when I had the chance. He was so gentle and sincere. He would never have hit me and we understood each other completely.

The first songs I wrote were about Adrian, and losing him. Emotionally charged, desolate and full of pining: it was my blue stage, all written in minor keys. My heart was broken and I saw no future for myself because all I had was this Music CSE and my dream of going to music college to become a professional musician was pie in the sky, even after praying every day for some miracle to happen. I needed O-levels and Grade 5 on two instruments, according to the books I found in the library. And I needed to apply to the Council for a grant for living costs. It was all out of my reach, academically.

I was stuck doing menial jobs. I had moved from the chemist to a dry cleaners, after Dad put in a word for me as he knew the owners, and I enjoyed being out of the house, but I certainly hated the feeling of doing work I had no interest in. Being in the shop also meant I was being asked out by boys and, because part of me wanted to be 'normal', I agreed. But after Adrian, it made me feel physically sick to be around these boys. They were nice – they bought me flowers, would take me to the cinema and my mother liked them all – but they did not smell like Adrian (it was his pheromones I craved) and they gave me the creeps. Although I never did, I wanted to punch them all when they tried to get physically close to me. I felt like I was being violated.

"You're absolutely awful, Karen," my mother told me once, arriving at my bedroom door with a bunch of red roses. "Look what this boy's bought you, and you don't want them. You can't even be bothered to come downstairs to see him."

"I don't like him, and I don't want them. You have them," I spat back. Adrian could have come with a dead daisy and I would have accepted it, but I was beginning to realise that that was never going to happen. My mother was trying her best to push me into a relationship, with the right sort of boy, but I was not interested. I suppose the boys saw me as playing hard to get which made them try harder – which, ironically, was the last thing I wanted.

All I did want was Adrian and if I could not have him, then I did not want anyone else: he is the reason I never married.

# MUSICAL AMBITIONS

THE door to musical college was closed to me, yet despite not finishing the hairdressing course I had been sent on while at St Georges', I still felt that hairdressing might be the next best thing. At least it would get me out of the dry cleaners where I had been wasting away for years and, after looking at Lewes College prospectus, I realised you did not need any school qualifications to get on a course.

But there was a problem. I would have to pay to enrol on the course as I was slightly over 19 years of age. Astonishingly, when I asked my parents for help, they said no. "You ruined your schooling, Karen," my mother said. "You've only got yourself to blame. We're not going to pay for college, and let you still live in this house rent free. If you go to college, where will your £5 a week keep come from? You've blown your chances."

I should have expected it really, but I was so shocked. I was trying to better myself, and I was hitting brick walls every step of the way. I was quite intelligent, yet I had not got the pieces of paper I needed and I was finding myself in menial jobs which were not stretching me and I was frustrated to say the least. I honestly thought I was going to be in prison before long, because I was bad and had no future.

Thankfully, however, I was made of sterner stuff than my parents realised and the manic side of my increasingly bipolar behaviour was actually a blessing at this time as I went on to fight my way into a musical career.

My first coup was persuading Dad to buy me a professional guitar, amplifier and other equipment, so I was £500 in debt to him. With my weekly earnings at the dry cleaners coming in at £19 a week, minus £5 keep, it was a long haul to pay him back, but I did, eventually. In my spare time I was playing electric guitar in a series of local bands, gigging to earn money. There was 'Lover Boy' first, in which I played for nine months, and then an all-girl band called 'Petticoat'. Girls playing electric guitar were gold in the music business at that time, with role models such as Suzi Quattro, Chrissie Hynde and Patti Smith, and 'Petticoat' could almost command its own fee. The band folded when one of the girls got pregnant and I suppose I was a bit of a pioneer playing electric guitar as I went on to form my own band, 'Mascara', but that did not last.

I was also giving guitar lessons and at Christmas I would take my pupils out carol singing for charity. And Karen (Head Girl at Chailey) would come with me. She was the only one who would tell me: "You're not a bad person. Deep down inside you're a very good person." It was amazing that she always kept such utter faith in me. I never believed her, of course.

It was a tough time, financially, for me as I was also having to pay for bus fares out of my earnings and I had no money for clothes, which was hard when I was trying to break into an industry which was dominated by image. Eventually I got a job in the evenings at a restaurant so I could save up and buy a car and have driving lessons. I needed to be mobile as I had been offered a place as rhythm guitarist with a group called 'Prohibition' and I later took over as bass player. I was pretty flexible musically and we performed at functions all over Sussex. All I wanted to do was turn professional and I continued to go for auditions, but the music business was so difficult. Thankfully, I was just so driven to succeed and I wanted to be like the musicians I admired: Barbara Dixon, Loretta Lynn and Carole King.

I was interviewed by the *Mid Sussex Times* local paper in July 1982, when I was just 20, and my overriding ambition seemed to be playing in the Ivy Benson band and having my own country band (country music suited my voice). In the article I say:

*"I have worked hard and I'm not going to give up now. It is a cut-throat business and there is a lot of drink and drugs around, but you have just got to keep your head and your eye on what you want… The music business is like a punch bag – every time it smashes you in the face, you smack it back twice as hard."*

How extraordinarily focused I was, and what a totally Karen Braysher thing to say. And what did I want the most, the journalist asked me. "To dedicate my first professional performance to the teachers at Chailey School who told me I wouldn't make it."

By September 10th, 1982 (two months after that article), I had met Ivy Benson, who had signed me into the Chiswick Working Man's Club where we had lunch. In a move which had precedent, I was so determined to reach Ivy Benson that I dropped a note through her letterbox in London, even though I did not expect to hear anything from her. I knew that if I hand-delivered the letter, at least she would be intrigued enough to read it. And I was right, because the next day I got a phone call and she asked me to come up for an audition and she took me to the Chiswick Club to perform a few songs in the afternoon. It was the most nerve-wracking moment in my life, but I knew this would be my only chance to achieve my ambition. Ivy took me on as a rhythm guitarist and country singer, but also to stand in on bass guitar (of which I then had no experience). It was such a big step to take, but I was more than ready to take the plunge. Ivy was well known for taking on girls like me, from troubled backgrounds, and bringing them on to be professional musicians. I played a few gigs with her and I grabbed this chance with both hands. She even asked me, in January 1983, to go with her to the Isle of Man and play the bass guitar. This was not my instrument, but she was going to find me a teacher to bring me up to speed.

# DAD GOES

DAD was so pleased for me when I got the offer from Ivy Benson to travel with her band. All this time he had been my roadie, lugging all my equipment along to each performance and waiting around for me to end, and he had seen how hard I had worked to get somewhere in music. He had also persuaded me to hand deliver my application form to the Saltdean hotel where I was hoping to do the Summer Season as a Butlin's Redcoat. I was tired of living at home, struggling financially, and decided that I would try to get into the entertainment industry for a brief run, rather than having all my eggs in one basket as a professional musician. And I am so glad Dad knew all about my blossoming career.

Unfortunately, the stomach ulcer which had initially driven him to Cornwall was still in the background and he was taking a tablet called Tagamet HB, which I knew cost £1 a tablet from when I worked in the chemists. He had been on it for years and years for heartburn but, unbeknown to us, the Tagamet was actually not doing his heart any good.

One morning in March 1983, only weeks before I was due to go to the Isle of Man with Ivy, Dad started to complain of chest pains. That night my friend, Henry, came over for supper and to watch a video, *Midnight Express* (not many people had video players then). Henry was a nice, very honest and local chap who I completely dominated. We had met while I briefly worked in the art department of the stationers and he kept coming in to buy single paint brushes until, eventually, he asked me out. When Henry left after watching the video, we arranged he would come over in the morning to go out for a run. Just before going to bed, I looked at my father and said, "Goodnight, Dad." It was something I would not normally have said, but some thought came into my mind. I was being warned.

"Your dad's having a heart attack!" was the next thing I heard, at five in the morning. Mum was in pieces and as I went downstairs I was not in the least bit surprised to find him on the sofa, with our lady doctor sitting by him. She had called Cuckfield Hospital to send an ambulance, but when they arrived they could not get the stretcher through the awkward doorway and during the struggle Dad had another heart attack. I remember my mother rushing out of the room as she was too terrified to watch, but I was strangely calm because I always think on the bright side. Even as one of the medics grabbed hold of Dad's ankles and dragged him onto the floor to start resuscitation, I was still hopeful. But there was nothing to be done, I soon realised, as the doctor took a torch and shined it in Dad's eyes. I looked at her, "He's dead, isn't he?" She got up and marched me out of the room to where my mother was standing in the sitting room. "He didn't make it," she confirmed to my mother. The reaction in Mum was weird – she just completely lost it.

I remained calm during the whole episode – I think I had been prepared the night before when I knew something would happen to Dad. I was the one who had to break the news over the phone to my brother and sister, and my sister was the first to arrive, shortly followed by the funeral directors. It was a Sunday morning and they came within the hour.

Then Henry turned up for the arranged run in his bright canary-yellow running tracksuit, jogging down the front path.

"Why aren't you ready, Karen?" he asked, between pants, looking at my pyjamas and slippers.

I was just numb. "I'm not coming."

"What? Don't let me down now; I've come all this way. Come on."

"I'm not doing it."

"I knew you'd dob out!"

"My dad's dead."

He stopped panting and stared. "What do you mean, your dad's dead? I was having dinner with your father last night."

"This morning. Heart attack."

He started to smile. "You're joking – just to get out of coming for a run."

I did not return the smile and I think the penny dropped for him.

I was so confused by my feelings, because when Dad eventually died one of my first thoughts was that I would never be hit again and I felt relief. I was free of his tempers and violence and I knew that I could live without fear now. But then the second thought I had was, "I forgive him, though, because it was not his fault. He was the bullet in my mother's gun." The feeling I was now left with was causing me to panic, "What am I going to do now, without him here?" I was left alone with my mother and Dad was an ally in a way, against Mum. Lorraine felt the same way. When she came down from her home in London, she was so upset and it was not just because we had lost our best buddy, in Dad, but the reality of what life would now be like with only our mother. But we still had each other.

I had only recently stepped in to help Lorraine, against Mum and Dad, and I am sure the stress of that episode, knowing what we then did about Tagamet, was the final nail in Dad's coffin. It had all started when Lorraine became an adult and left Chailey School and the transition home in Newhaven. Her future was in Dad and Mum's hands and they continually argued about where to send Lorraine. Lorraine's choice was John Grooms in London, which was a Christian centre, focusing on the arts, but she was in a local 'Cheshire Home' which was really a nursing home, in which she was sharing a bedroom with an elderly lady, who was incontinent. The Thalidomide Trust had given our parents a car to use to visit Lorraine, but they did not like driving long distances so they were looking for somewhere suitable for her to move to, but locally. This was causing long, drawn-out, and increasingly bitter, arguments. Eventually, Lorraine was moved to Wood Larks, in Kent, but while it was a beautiful, rural location with modern wood buildings, all the other inhabitants had either learning difficulties, or were more disabled than her, so with no one to talk to it was a lonely place for her to be.

When we visited her there, I was so shocked about the change in my normally bubbly sister. She was very dumbed down, almost numb. I think she was just very depressed and when I managed to get her on my own, I said, "What do you want me to do?"

She turned and looked me straight in the eyes. "Promise me, Karen, you'll get me out of here. Please get me out of here."

"I'll do everything I can, Lorraine, I promise you."

"I want to go to John Grooms in London. That's where all the other Thalidomiders are. It's the place I want to go. I don't want to be here; I don't belong here."

"Don't worry," I whispered to her. "I'll not let you down. I promise I'll get you out of here."

As we drove away that afternoon, I looked out of the back window to see Lorraine forlornly sitting in her wheelchair with tears running down her cheeks. I wiped my tears away and knew exactly what I was going to do next. I badgered my parents non-stop.

"Lorraine wants to go to John Grooms."

"No, she's not going there. That's in Edgware, North London, and we're not driving all that way to go and see her."

"But you've got a Trust car and that's what that's for, to drive and see Lorraine."

"That's none of your business."

"It is my business." And you can imagine the arguments were rolling along. Every opportunity I had, I put forward Lorraine's case to move. Even when they were arguing between themselves, I would interject – "Lorraine wants to go to John Grooms."

I made a complete pain of myself, but there was no way I was going to give up as I had promised Lorraine and once I got something in my head – this was the undiagnosed bipolar again – I could not let it go. Drive my point. Drive my point. Drive my point home. Then one breakfast time, I snapped. I had some cornflakes in a round bowl and I was going on and on and on about John Grooms, and I got myself into such a state that I threw the bowl at my father, like it was a frisbee. He ducked and the milk and cornflakes hit the wall and fell, with the fractured bowl, onto the floor. I ran out of the room as fast as I could because I did not want another beating, but I think that force of feeling must have impressed Dad and in the end, miraculously, Lorraine got to John Grooms. But at what cost to Dad's health?

But at the time, I was so happy for Lorraine and when we went to visit her in London she was so excited to be back with her friends that when I got out of the car she rushed towards me in her wheelchair, propelling herself along with crutches under her little arms. She pushed so hard, without her safety belt done up, that she fell straight out of her wheelchair onto the drive and smashed her teeth. The next minute she was off in an ambulance and she returned later that afternoon, all numbed but ecstatically happy to be in the place which was right for her.

If I think about Dad now I still get a tear in my eye (this is many years after counselling). I did not grieve for him when I first lost him, but, my God, I did as I grew older. Part of me feels guilty for the stress I put on Dad. I had many problems and I had this incessant determination to get things done, but my overriding anger still lies with my mother. She contributed to his early death and she set him off on his violent rages. I think she killed him.

And when she had killed him, she left me in a 500-year old cottage, with the cat. She took the dog and went to live with her father, of all people. I think she had a breakdown, but nothing was ever said. I was also not in a good place, having lost Dad. I was terrified of being in the house on my own. It was full of pain and ghosts after Dad had died there. Luckily, I had Henry to rely on and for the first few nights he slept on the settee downstairs (we never had sex – too frightened of getting pregnant). I was desperate not to be alone. I even slept on a lilo in my sister's lounge to get away from the house. Henry's parents asked if I would like to stay with them and I jumped at the chance.

I cannot remember having any contact with my mother while she was away; my brother told me she was ill and needed some space. I was the last one she would have wanted to see, but I did feel abandoned by her, even though part of me was relieved not to have her around. I had to grow up quickly and I decided to run away from my grief; to leave home.

Losing Dad, at that particular career crossroads in my life, made only one option stand out. Butlin's offered me a live-in contract as a Redcoat for the Summer 1983 season and I was ready to take it. I rang Ivy Benson and explained about the offer, it being close to home after Dad dying, and she advised me to grasp the opportunity. "Take it. Take it because you are a good entertainer and they'll bring you on. Come back to me when you've done your time there. I wholeheartedly let you go to do that. I think it's the right thing to do." I so badly needed to hear her positivity and I was slightly relieved as well, because I would have had to learn a new instrument for Ivy and I was unsure how I would cope with that, and also with sight-reading of a musical score.

I had Ivy's blessing, but there was someone in my way. My mother. She was back and forth from her father's house, breaking up the house contents ready to sell our home. It was too big for her now, and she wanted to move into the town to be near my sister. "You should be staying here with me, looking after me now Dad's gone, Karen. It's the very least you could do, after all the trouble you've caused." And my sister was saying the same thing. I was beginning to teeter about becoming a Redcoat. It felt so unfair that at long last I was finally getting the break I wanted, to get on in life, and I was being put under an almighty guilt trip to stay and look after a mother who I hated.

Then into my life walked one of my heroes. Mr Mack. He owned the corner shop over the road from my sister's house and I was sent on an errand by Sue, when I was working with her. I walked into his shop and he said to me, "I understand your father's died."

"Yeah."

"It must be making you sad."

"It is a bit," I said and carried on, airing my woes. "The worst thing is that Sue and my mother seem to think that because I'm not married that I should stay at home and look after her."

He immediately went to the door and put the 'Closed' sign up in the window. He turned to me. "You listen to me. Just because you're the only one not married, it doesn't mean to say you have to give up your life. Let me give you a word of warning." And he went on to tell the whole story of how the spinster stays at home and looks after the elderly mother and stays there her whole life. I listened intently to this man I hardly knew. "And your father would not want you to stay at home. He would want you to get out there and make the most of your life."

With that, he turned the 'Open' sign over and carried on with his work. I left the shop and made my mind up to go to Butlin's. He was right. Dad would have not wanted me to mope about at home, looking after my mother.

"What took you so long, Karen?" asked Sue, as I returned to help her with her hairdressing (she had a little salon in her kitchen).

"Oh nothing – just had a chat with Mr Mack."

My decision to become a Redcoat was heavily criticised, but I was determined and I took to entertaining like a duck to water.

# BUTLIN'S

AND so began the first of many manic periods in my life. I was on a complete high. Three months after Dad died, I started as a General Redcoat on 14th May, 1983, with non-negotiable hours, six days on and one day off, for £57.75 a week. Initially, I was put in a room on my own in the guest quarters of the Ocean Hotel at Saltdean (now a block of flats) as the General Manager knew I had been recently bereaved and I was the only female singer of the team. I was being taken care of, and it was the best possible place for me to be for several reasons.

I was thrown in straight away, with a week-long training course. We were taught how to put on make-up properly, how to ballroom dance (we were encouraged to dance with the guests), deportment and how to speak properly (I was fine with that as I had a 'posh' Sussex voice). It was like being in the Army and the regimented regime kept me both busy and, rather surprisingly, I responded well to being told what to do. "Kaz (as I was known), you're too inhibited," Mrs Conner, the Entertainments' Manager, barked at me. It was the first time I had spoken in to a microphone and I was petrified of hearing my voice so loud, but instead of reacting badly to authority, I kept on trying and eventually you could not get me off the microphone during the evening's entertainments.

I was only late once and was given 5am stage cleaning duty as punishment. I duly set my alarm clock, donned my track suit and spent half an hour washing and scrubbing the stage. It was ridiculous, but I was never late again.

We had a very strict policy on uniform, which I never argued with, which was strange as all those years at school and all I wanted to do was wear jewellery and rubbish any dress code. One of the greatest lessons I learnt was early on. I had reported to breakfast duty in what I thought was the correct uniform. "You're not dressed properly, Kaz," said the manager.

"Oh?"

"Go back to your room, look in the mirror and see what's missing."

So I did. But I could not see anything wrong. I had clean white shoes, the starched collar, the perfectly pleated skirt, hair tidy. What could be missing? I returned back to the breakfast room.

"No, you're still not dressed properly," he told me again. "Go back."

By this time, my patience was wearing thin, but I returned to my room. Still could not see the problem. Returned.

I was defeated. "Please tell me what's wrong with the way I'm dressed."

"Where is your smile this morning, Kaz? You're never fully dressed without a smile!"

How did I manage to keep my temper under control in the face of this 'provocation'? I just knew I needed to keep this job. I wanted a career and I knew this was one of my last chances. I had to get it right and I would do nothing to put that in jeopardy.

Of course, I still questioned authority when I felt someone deserved it and the Head Redcoat, also called Karen (hence I was called Kaz), came in for some mild banter because she had no talent and was only interested in how starched our collars were and whether we were turned out smartly.

Butlin's was also wonderful because suddenly I had people of my own age around me, and it was the first time I had ever felt part of a big family. The contrast of my huge, joy-filled 21st birthday to my depressing 18th birthday in the pub with only my parents showed how far my life had come, socially. I had been excluded from school, lost touch with my friends, been surrounded by shouting and aggression at home and here I now was, in a gang with people from all sorts of backgrounds, having the best time. I was learning how to interact with people and we were all so busy, working all hours, but loving it, that my manic personality did not seem out of the ordinary – I blended in perfectly.

On a personal level, I became a more rounded entertainer and, with practise, I found it easy to cope with the big audiences I was in front of. While I was on the stage, singing and playing my guitar, I grew in confidence and learnt all the skills I needed: how to address people, how to have eye contact with the audience, how to manipulate an audience and how to engage with people. I learnt to play the banjo and did old-time musical singalong sessions, as there was no karaoke at the time, and I had my own country music spot which I would do with band backing.

I also found another hidden strength within me. During one Redcoat meeting, one of my male colleagues made a joke about a Thalidomider running across the road and, instead of reacting badly, I stood up in the room and calmly talked about Lorraine. The room went quiet and you could have heard a pin drop. I amazed myself by staying calm, and I just told everyone the truth about Lorraine and her condition and answered their subsequent questions. I accepted my colleague's apology and that was probably the point when I realised that it was possible for me to articulate my deep worries and concerns to my peer group, without making them angry and, in turn, without making myself angry. Butlin's, being a caring and supportive environment, gave me the chance to live a normal life, or as normal as a nearly 24hrs-a-day life in entertainment can be.

I never went to Butlin's with any other focus than to help my career, but in several ways my new-found freedom in Saltdean saw me experiment with other ways of living and being: spiritually and sexually.

When Dad first died, my local parish vicar had totally confused me when I went to see him about Dad's funeral, because when I started to cry he said, "There's no need for crying. It's only your father's overcoat which has died." I totally missed his meaning and when I got home I stood in front of Dad's coat hanging in the hall and could not understand, because the coat was still there. It was not until a few months later when I was working as a Redcoat that a woman came up to me one night and totally surprised me.

"I'm a medium," she said, "and I can see a middle-aged man standing next to you. Very close to you. He's very protective of you. Have you lost your father, dear?"

"Yes, I have"

"Well, he's very close to you, dear."

And I actually felt him around me. I had no spiritualist knowledge, never read any books and yet I still felt this presence around me. Eventually, I shared my thoughts with my roommate, Sally, a 'Peggy Spencer' dancer.

"Do you think there is life after death?"

"Well, I've heard that there's such places as Spiritualist churches."

"Are there?" I asked. "What do they do there?"

"I think you can get messages through from dead people."

"Oh!"

"We ought to look to see if there's one in Brighton," she suggested.

After looking in the phone book, we decided that Sunday would be my chance to get a message from Dad. But I was petrified walking into the Brighton National Spiritualist Church, because I imagined it would be full of ghosts and Dad would be sitting in a pew waiting for me. Of course, there were no pews, only rows of seats, there was no stained-glass windows or an altar, and certainly no visible spectres.

"Should we stay?" I whispered to Sally, as we sheepishly took our seats.

She nodded, "We might as well."

We sat there waiting. "When do you think the ghosts will come out?" I asked.

But then the organist started to play and everyone started to sing and clap. We went along with it. Then these people came down the aisle, dressed in their Sunday best, and the woman in the group welcomed us. We sang other hymns, which I had not heard of before, and there was a healing prayer said, where those present could send the special powers of healing to friends or relatives.

Sally and I nudged each other; we were completely overwhelmed by the whole experience and confused. We were waiting for the messages to come through, but it seemed that we would have to wait for the good bit until the end as next up was the visiting medium who gave an address – with philosophical, rather than religious, content. Finally, the woman leading the service said,

"And now Ladies and Gentlemen, we will ask our friend to stand up and connect with loved ones in the spirit world."

Sally and I looked at each other. The lady came to this woman, that man, giving out information – tears were shed, nods were given in response to questions.

"Bloody hope she doesn't come to me," I whispered. It was all too frightening. We came away with no messages – thankfully – but something odd had happened to me.

A few days later, Sally and I were with another Redcoat, Linda, talking about the spiritualist church experience, when for some reason I took Linda's hand in my palms and I immediately started to see pictures in my head. When I closed my eyes, the images played out like a movie scene and I just started describing what I was seeing. The pictures stopped and I opened my eyes to see Linda with tears rolling down her cheeks. "Oh, my goodness, what's the matter? Have I said anything to upset you?"

"No, Karen. I just can't believe it – you were absolutely bang on with what you said. How on earth did you do that?"

I had no idea, but I knew I was exhausted. Word quickly spread and I was asked to do more palm reading, even by the guests. I would sit at their table in the Ballroom, in the evenings, and they would offer me money, but I did not want paying as I was worried if I took money, my 'power' might dry up. In the end, I was not allowed to do the reading in public as Sir Billy Butlin did not like 'black magic', so I knocked it off.

Also I had become aware of my father's presence around me – he would be with me in the car, in my room with me and I got quite upset about it. I was not scared of him, as I had been when he was alive, but I was never on my own. He was always there; just behind me. He never left me alone. It got to the point that I could not go to bed at night because I was worried there would be a ghost at the end of the bed.

Eventually, I told my brother about the palm reading and that Dad would not leave me alone. "Well," he replied, "if Dad is there, you should tell him to go away and be where he needs to be, but not with you. He mustn't linger with you. If you tell him that, he won't trouble you any more." I do not think my brother believed me; he was a policeman used to dealing with delusional people and probably thought my grief was turning me slightly mad. But I was just getting sensitive to the spiritual world and when I did ask my father to leave me alone, he did. He vanished. And so did my ability to read palms. I had had my introduction to spiritualism but it had frightened me too much. Many years later I was to return to the world, but back then I had only just suffered bereavement and I was no way ready, in any shape or form, to accept a new way of life, a new way of being. I was too vulnerable and my brother did the right thing, being sensitive and practical.

With Spiritualism now on the back burner, something else happened at Butlin's which completely took me by surprise and turned my life upside down. I was still friendly with Henry and we used to hook up occasionally, but there was no sexual element to our relationship and, to be honest, I was stretching my wings and I had lost interest in him. I was having too much fun in my off-duty time with my new friends, and especially with Andrew, one of my fellow Redcoats.

"Come on, Kaz – let's go for a drive," he would say to me. I had my Dad's car – a green Talbot – and I would take Andrew down to Brighton along the seafront. Every time we went he would get caught short down at Madeira Drive.

"Pull over, would you, Kaz? I'll be back in a sec; dying to go to the loo."

So, I would stop the car and wait for him. And wait for him.

"You've been gone ages," I would say to him on his return.

"Yeah, sorry about that. There was a queue."

"What? At this time of night?"

I only found out what he was doing at the end of Summer Season party when this policemen came over to dance with me. All my friends thought this guy fancied me because he would come to every cabaret performance I did on a Wednesday night – I had not noticed him, but everyone else had. Finally, he asked me to dance after my show. I was not interested in him at all and I found him pretty creepy, but I agreed to dance because my bosses were watching and you had to dance with guests.

As we danced, he said to me: "I've been watching you all summer."

"Oh?" I asked.

"Yes, I've been watching where you take your car late at night."

My goodness, he has got a crush on me; he's been following me, I thought.

"Down at Madeira Drive. You wait there for ages."

"Yeah. I wait for my friend, Andrew."

"I know," said the policeman. "Don't do it again."

"What? Why?" I asked, innocently.

"Because I like you and I don't want you to get mixed up in Andrew's world because if you carry on, you'll be arrested. You are his taxi driver and he goes cottaging there."

I did not understand a word he was saying and when the music finished I made my excuses and left him standing on the dance floor. I went to find Andrew.

Andrew laughed when I told him. "Yeah, sorry, Kaz, you're the only one with a car!"

This was the first time I had even really thought about sexuality. I was shocked when I found out what Andrew had been up to and realised how innocent I was to everything like that. I was still a virgin, because of the fear of getting pregnant, and I generally did not like boys, or men – no one except for Adrian. Andrew had often commented that I was a closet gay because over the summer I had cut my hair short and started to wear butch clothes.

"Oh, don't be ridiculous!" I would say. "What rubbish!"

Anyway, I was in complete awe of the eccentric piano tuner who turned up once to sort out the grand piano in the Ballroom – there was no way I was gay. This man played Mozart and Chopin to an empty and echoing room; it was such an incredibly magical moment and he stole my heart. He wore this funny suit and had very small round glasses, with mad hair and his voice was so posh and his mannerisms were larger than life.

I was so taken with him that I said, "Would you like a pot of tea?" Not a cup of tea, but a pot, and I rushed up to the canteen to get supplies and I sat pouring this tea for him while in rapture. I could hear occasional giggles from my colleagues behind the curtains as they saw the hilarious sight of me falling for the mad pianist. But I loved eccentric and interesting people; I was so attracted to him. Henry and the creepy policeman were nothing to me.

Once the policeman and other party guests had gone, we had a photo taken of all the Redcoats and staff at the hotel. There was one receptionist, Lynn, who was so drunk that Andrew suggested we take her down to our bedrooms in the hotel basement to sleep it off. It was against the rules as off-site staff had to be off the premises by 11pm, but it was the end of the season and it would do no harm.

"You can stay in my room," I said to Lynn, as my roommate had already left, and I steered her to the spare bed and she slumped down in a heap. I was still hyped after the party so I put on a record and made myself some coffee.

"Want some?" I asked Lynn.

We sat and chatted about her twin sister, who she lived with, and the fact that she was 13 years older than me. Then she leaned towards me, "I've always fancied you, you know."

"Really?" I just could not believe it. What was I supposed to do with this information?

I knew that I felt comfortable being around her (I certainly did not want to thump her, which I usually felt when a man approached me), but I did not know what to do or what to think.

In the morning, Lynn had to go up to work a shift, but she asked if she could see me again. "Yes, of course." Lynn arrived a while later with a tray of breakfast for me. Breakfast in bed. That was the first time anyone had done that for me and I was so taken aback. We never even touched that night or morning, but I knew that something had changed in me. Perhaps it was Lynn showing me such kindness, because I had never known such kindness from an older female. I wanted to grab this feeling with both hands and despite neither Lynn or I having been in a gay relationship before, we started getting close.

However, there was a difficulty with this. Lynn was support staff and I was a Redcoat – like an officer – and we were not supposed to mix off duty. But I started to flout the rules for her.

# CRASH LANDING

ON my days off, I would go back to Wivelsfield, just for a few hours, and be greeted by the sight of Mum and Sue packing up the cottage. Mum either sold off or gave away most of Dad's things (including all his photographic equipment which he left to me in his will) and it was heartbreaking seeing the swimming pool being closed down, and packing boxes everywhere. Eventually, my mother sold up and moved into a semi-detached house in the same road as Sue in Haywards Heath and I ended up staying on at Butlin's for the Winter Season because I could not face going 'home'.

During this time, the hotel was busy during the weekends, when guests would stay from Friday to Monday, but during the weekdays I would jump on a coach with my fellow band members and go to these big companies, like Ford in Dagenham, to play a gig to promote Butlin's holidays. I was the band's guitarist and, because I had never played in such a band before, I got lessons from the band leader, Simon. I was never paid to be the guitarist as there was no budget, but I learnt so many skills and had such a fun time going out and about. My experience in the band also meant that I was called upon to play in the late night Cabaret Show back at the hotel (when the regular guitarist came off duty at 11pm).

After the Show, that winter, I would sit and have drinks with the guests and Lynn would occasionally appear, already quite inebriated. "Come up to the staff bar and have a drink with me?" she would ask.

"But I can't be seen up there. I'm not allowed."

"Oh, suit yourself," Lynn would say, flouncing off.

Just a quick one wouldn't hurt, I would think and follow her at a safe distance.

In the bar, she would order me a large drink and wink, handing it to me: "That's for services rendered." I had not got a clue what she meant by this – I was completely naive – but I enjoyed her company, even though it was so risky for us to socialise. She was showing me kindness, and she was the forbidden fruit.

I am not sure whether people began to realise what was going on between us, but I remember one day being in the rehearsal room with others, singing *Will you still love me tomorrow?*, when there was a knock on the door and Lynn's face appeared at the window. "It's your friend, Kaz. Get rid of her and make it snappy," said Karen, the Head Redcoat.

"Lynn, what do you want?" I asked her, hurriedly. "I can't come now."

"I want to see you later," she told me, absolutely pissed, and leaning against the door threatening to fall through it.

"You can't come in here," I said, pushing her away. "We're rehearsing."

"I just want to see you, Karen. Is that a crime?"

"No, no. But I can't come now. I'll come and find you as soon as we're done."

"Really?" she asked, crestfallen.

"Yes, of course. Go and wait for me in my room."

With Lynn gone, I went back into the rehearsal room. "You shouldn't invite people like that here, Kaz. You know the rules."

"Yes, yes, I know, but I didn't ask her to come and she's probably had too much drink."

I did go and see Lynn later, just to pacify her, and we were playing music until late, way past the kicking out time of 11pm. Someone must have heard us because there was a knock at the door and two burly security men stood in the doorway.

"Right, you," one said, looking past me at Lynn, "Out. You know the rules. You're not a live-in member of staff. You're not authorised to be down here, and you," he turned to look at me, "shouldn't have let her stay. You both know the rules. I'll be going to HR in the morning to report you."

I was stunned. Lynn gathered her things and was escorted off the premises. Someone must have grassed me up.

The next morning I was called up to HR and told to pack my

bags and leave. I was sacked for letting Lynn be in my room after 11pm. I could not believe it. "But who's sacked me?" I asked.

"Your line manager, Simon."

Now, Simon was the new Entertainments' Manager who was the same Simon I played with in the band. I marched off to find him – my temper was high. I could not believe the unfairness of it.

"Well, thanks very much, Simon! For all the hard work I've put in over the Summer and Winter seasons and now you're going to sack me just like that?" I shouted.

"Well, Kaz, you knew the rules, didn't you?"

"Yes, but…"

"Listen," he said, trying to calm me down. "Your time is done here, Kaz. You've come to the end. Your time is done. You must leave."

I cried so much over the next few hours. My whole world was imploding – I had lost my job, my home, my (girl)friend and I had to go to my mother's house and ask her if I could stay. But as I left, standing in tears at the staff quarter's door, one of the Redcoats called Husk came over to me: "There's a big world out there, Kaz. Go and find it."

I looked up at him, and could only raise a weak smile. I was going back to the hornet's nest.

I found myself living in an alien environment. I was used to large, detached rural houses and now I found myself in a poky little house in town. "This is my house and my rules and you will live by them," she told me as soon as I came off the street.

What on earth was I going to do now? Where was I going to go? I knew I could not stay with my mother for long, but I was in such shock that I was temporarily paralysed. My only clear thought, in my mania, was that I must see Lynn. Lynn became my rock. She would want me. She would look after me.

I phoned her house and spoke to Jane, her twin. Jane and Lynn had been brought up by their grandmother in Herefordshire and Jane, in particular, had a real country bumpkin accent. "Lynn ain't 'ere," she told me. I panicked. Where was she? It was because of her that I had been sacked. She could not just clear off.

It turned out that Lynn had lost her job too and when I caught up with her she was living in a dive of a bed and breakfast in Brighton, on the dole. She had a dark, damp basement room with a sash window that could not be locked, so after our first meeting I would just come down the basement steps, pull up the window and climb in over the bed and into the room. We went out in Brighton a few times for drinks and we began to build a proper relationship. I fell in love with her and she fell in love with me.

It was the biggest secret I had ever had because there was no way that I could tell my mother, or sister. It was between Lynn and me, and no one else. However, Jane found out. I will never forget when she met me and Lynn in a coffee shop in Brighton and she asked outright, "Well, is this 'ere a full-on relationship?"

I looked at Lynn, horrified. "She knows?" I asked Lynn. She replied with a nod.

Jane continued: "Because I've taken Lynn down to Family Planning, and asked 'em whether this thing you 'ave is 'cos Lynn don't want to get pregnant. Is that the reason YOU'RE doing it?" she stared at me, hoping to get a positive response.

I had to disappoint her.

"No, no. I love Lynn, that's all. Nothing to do with not getting pregnant." I almost laughed it was such a comical suggestion.

"And does your mother know about this?"

"Certainly not!"

"Well, I think there's something wrong with Lynn and you, and I'm going to take her back down to Family Planning to see if they can give her anything."

"Give her anything for what?" I asked.

"To stop her getting pregnant so she won't have to carry on with you. Lynn tells me it's only feelings – nothing physical involved."

I spluttered into my coffee.

"No, Jane, I'm afraid I have to tell you there is." Lynn glared at me, then put her hands over her face.

"Oh my God," said Jane, turning towards her sister. "You told me there was nothing physical. Now, I'm definitely taking you down Family Planning."

There was so much ignorance about homosexuality back in 1984. I was 21 and Lynn was 34. I remember Andrew had come into the Redcoat Common Room and shown us a leaflet he had been given at a nightclub in Brighton about Terrence Higgins. It was a time of uncertainty and this awful disease, HIV, was claiming the lives of same-sex partners and condoms were being handed out as protection. Were Lynn and I at risk? Could you catch HIV from kissing or off toilet seats? There were no public information films or hard research.

And if Brighton was just starting to be open about HIV and same-sex relationships, then Haywards Heath was a backwater and any mention of 'lesbian' was taboo. There was no way I was going to be open with my family.

It was bad enough living with my mother, without my secret being known. The rules at her house were so strict: aged 21, I had to be home by 10pm and if I was late it would cause huge arguments. I began to really hate my mother, all over again. I did not have enough money to support myself, as I was only working weekends with Henry at a garden centre. My new love, Lynn, was living in a hovel so I could not move in with her and after staying with her on Saturday nights I was always late for work on Sundays. Against this personal confusion and grief, there was the Miners' Strikes which my brother, David, was drafted up country to deal with, The Grand Hotel in Brighton was bombed (luckily, Lynn, who worked there, was with me that night) and HIV was spreading amongst the gay community.

It was then the depression came rolling in and I just could not stop crying. From the high mania of Butlin's, I came back down to earth – hard.

"We've noticed that you're not yourself lately," my mother said to me. "We think there's something wrong," she added, nodding towards Sue who was studying me carefully. It was nice of them to have noticed my tears – buckets of tears, more like – but I was wary of what was coming next.

"Are you going out with a black man?" my mother asked, accusingly.

"No. Where did you get that idea from?" I replied.

"Oh, we just thought that might be the reason for all your secrecy – coming in late at night, moping about, crying. You know we wouldn't tolerate you being with a black man."

There. I knew it. They were not concerned for me.

"Are you on drugs, then?" asked my sister.

I shook my head. There was no way I was going to let them know about Lynn. She was my precious secret and I longed to be with her, away from all this.

"Are you pregnant?" continued Sue.

"Ah, yes! You must be – that explains the moping around!" said Mum.

"No. No, I'm not pregnant."

"Are you a lesbian?" Sue asked.

Option number four. Lesbian.

I could not help it. I started to cry.

"I knew it. I knew it, Sue. I knew there was something wrong. She's a lesbian!" shrieked my mother, her voice getting louder. She peered at me. "I can only imagine what you get up to. All those late nights and 'sleep-overs' on a Saturday.

"Right, Sue, what do you think? Should we take her to the doctors? Get an appointment with Dr Young. We'll go and see if the doctor can give you something to stop you being… like this."

Sue nodded.

That night I began to think about what they had said. Was I really ill? Was my loving Lynn an illness that could be 'corrected'? Would that mean I would not love Lynn any more? My goodness, I was so confused. Being with Lynn felt so natural, yet now I had it in my head that perhaps I really was ill.

The next day I was frogmarched to my doctor's appointment, but made to sit outside while my mother went in to see Dr Young alone. After five minutes she came to get me. "Get in there," she hissed.

I went in to the room alone, worried about what might happen next.

Dr Young invited me to sit down.

I sat down.

"Your Mum's quite upset, isn't she?"

"Yes."

"Well, I have to tell you, Karen, that there's absolutely nothing wrong with you."

"Really…? I thought there was."

"No, there really is nothing wrong with you. Having feelings for another woman is perfectly natural – you're certainly not ill. But I think you and your mother should have some counselling together."

So, this counsellor eventually came to talk to us at home about the spectrum of sexuality and explained that my lesbianism was perfectly normal. "And I love, Lynn," I said, finishing the discussion. But my mother was having none of it. She was perfectly happy when I said I was off to Ibiza for the summer, working as a holiday rep, because I was parted from Lynn.

# SOLO CAREER

IN April 1984, I had started to apply for work in the resorts for the Summer Season. I was so glad Ivy Benson had told me to go to Butlin's because, with that experience behind me, I could now apply for any job in holiday entertainment. I was offered a contact with all the major holiday camps, but the most exciting job came with Club Rendezvous, owned by Mecca, out in Ibiza as Head of Entertainments. Finally, I could start earning decent money to get out of my mother's jail and move with Lynn to a decent place.

"I'm going to get a roof over our heads, Lynn," I told her. She was not happy with me going abroad for the Summer, especially surrounded by the temptation of other 18-30 year olds. "I won't even look at them," I said as reassurance.

And I did not. I hated that job. There was all sorts of alcohol and drug abuse and I spent quite a bit of my time retrieving guests from police cells and looking after them. I was completely out of my comfort zone as I was used to a Butlin's family audience, rather than being an 'adult minder'. I lasted two months.

Apart from the work, I was also unhappy without Lynn. I really only felt complete when I was with her. I was phoning her a lot, but saying 'I miss you' and hearing the same from Lynn was not enough for me – I was pining to be with her. In the end, I did not think I was earning enough money to warrant my feeling so sad, depressed and hopeless about the job and being away from Lynn. So, I transferred to Sinah Warren, on Hayling Island, as a Greencoat.

But that did me no good, either. The place was more upmarket and professional than Butlin's and I felt rather out of my depth in terms of my singing and the activities I was supposed to be taking part in (archery and horse riding). I just could not be bothered with it all and I did not have the energy to do another Summer

Season. Depression was sapping me. And Simon's words came flooding back to me: "Your time is done here, Kaz. You've come to the end." I called a taxi one afternoon, gathered all my belongings together and left a note in my room for the roommate to find. Took the taxi to the train station. From Portsmouth to Haywards Heath. Went to the phone box. Called Mum.

Sitting in her house that evening, I decided that now was the time to build my own career as a solo artist and although I did not know how I was going to do it, I was adamant that was the way to support myself and Lynn.

I went to see Lynn the next day and we got back together, despite her telling me that Jane had been trying to set her up with men while I had been away in Ibiza and Hayling Island. Jane, like my mother, was adamant that Lynn and I were not right in the head; we had an illness, a hormone imbalance perhaps, and we needed help. Mum even tried to offer money to Lynn to leave me alone: "Name your price," she had said. Part of me did believe Sue and Mum – that I was ill. There was certainly a torment going on in my mind when I was away from Lynn, pulling me away from her. They would point out my erratic and aggressive behaviour at school, my mood swings during my periods and my constant tears: loving Lynn could just be part of my illness. How prophetic that was, without any of us realising it.

I started my solo career by doing a gig in the pub – The Spanish Lady – which was next to the Butlin's hotel in Saltdean. I had bought myself a small drum machine to give a bigger sound, rather than just me and my guitar, but it was difficult to practise as Mum's neighbour kept going on about the noise. Eventually, I had enough songs to cover an evening and I invited my Redcoat friends, including Simon, to support me. The place was buzzing, being Summer, and the night went beyond my expectations. I realised then that I was confident in front of an audience and in time I bought a really good PA system, with money from Dad's will, and I got taken on by a couple of agents.

I pounded the streets getting gigs. I was so determined to get my own place so I could live with Lynn. I went out to social clubs, pubs and factories, armed with contracts from the Musician's Union and Equity, with the goal of coming away with five bookings every day. That was my target. Sometimes I would take my mother along (it was a day out for her and occasionally we got along) because I thought people might take me more seriously and it worked. I hit my targets. I even did a three-week pub tour all over London in Friary Meux pubs which was a real learning curve. I was building on my Butlin's experience and studying audiences. What could I get away with? What worked? What did not? I learnt the importance of eye contact with an audience and discovered some tricks to work people's subconscious to my advantage.

I was so desperate to get away from home that my determination was huge. I started to earn quite good money, on average £35 to £40 a night, and was building a successful gig circuit. I also took on a couple of cleaning jobs during the week to add to the 'Get Away Fund'.

My finances started improving at just the right time. One winter's night, I came in at 2am, having been out gigging in the cold, and I tiptoed upstairs as if I were a mouse. I was so quiet.

"I CAN HEAR YOU!" shouted my mother, through her bedroom door which was slightly ajar. "YOU'RE OUT OF HERE TOMORROW."

Next morning we continued the argument. "You can pack your bags and leave," she said.

"But I've got nowhere to go."

"That is not my problem."

I just stood still, at a loss. How was I supposed to convince her that her rules were ridiculous?

Then she grabbed my hand and bent my fingers back. She was towering over me as I fell to my knees in pain.

"Stop doing that. You're hurting me."

But she carried on, bending my fingers so far back that they started to crack. I thought she would break my hand.

"Stop! I'm a musician. I play guitar. Stop!"

"I will stop," she shouted, "if you apologise for being a lesbian!"

Somehow I managed to get away from her, and I cannot remember if I actually apologised to get away, but at that point I was quite happy to leave. I hated her. I resented her. This was not just her house. Dad had provided for her and me. This was my house, too. Yet I was being treated, aged 21, as a child – her and her ridiculous rules.

I ran upstairs and gathered all my belonging, even the pot plants, and piled them into my car. I then met Sue in the street, obviously having been summoned by our mother. "Good riddance," she happily joined in to the squalid fight. "That's it, Mum, you kick her out. She's never been any good."

"I'm going to for sure, Sue, don't you worry about that! And, Karen, don't you think about going crying to your Auntie Daphne, either. She won't want to know you now, not when she hears what you've turned in to. She'll cross the street if she sees you and she'll never talk to you again. In fact, none of the aunties or cousins will speak to you ever again."

I was crying when the phone rang and it was Mrs Thompson, the bank manager's wife. "Will you be coming to clean today, Karen, you are rather late?"

I could not get the words out easily, through my sobs.

"Mrs Thompson, I can't come because my mother's in the throes of kicking me out."

"Oh," she replied. "I've phoned at a bad time. Hopefully, we'll see you another day."

I put the phone down. Something in me snapped.

Mum was behind me. I turned round to face her. "You know what?" I shouted, "When you die, I'll spit on your grave." And with that, I walked out of the house. But she was not going to be beaten. She stood on the door step and called out, "And you owe me £15 keep."

I managed to find my purse and I threw it at her.

"And the keys?" she said with a final flourish.

I took the keys out of my bag and threw them into the snow which had fallen during the night. "Get them yourself."

I left that evening with only £100 to my name, in a Post Office savings account.

I drove to my Nan's house, just down the road, to get some support. There was nowhere else to go. I could not tell her the real reason I had been thrown out because I did not want to fall out with her too, but she would not let me stay. "I don't want Brenda storming round here if I let you stay. I'm sorry, darling, but you can leave your things here if you want."

Poor Nellie. She was stuck in the middle of waring relations.

I unpacked my car at Nan's and belted down to Brighton to see Lynn. "I've been kicked out," I told her.

"Good."

Suddenly, my resolve returned. "I'm going to find a better B&B for us and I'll let you know how I get on."

So, I returned to Haywards Heath and looked through the adverts. "I only take men," said the owner of one in Millgreen Road, near to the station.

"But my mum's thrown me out and I've got nowhere to sleep tonight."

There was a pause. "Well, you'd better come round and see me then."

And that was how Woody came into my life. Another of my heroes.

I think I was a broken woman at that point. Emotionally wounded. And, although Lynn moved in with me to the B&B, I really could not hold anything together. I could not do cleaning jobs and I could only manage a few gigs because I was mentally all over the place and I had nowhere to practise. Even listening to music, which had always pulled me through before, was no help.

I felt safe with Lynn, though, and when she was around (and sober) I was totally happy. It was the first time that someone, since Adrian, had shown me kindness and love and I lapped it up. And even though living in the B&B was difficult, I could be with Lynn. We had no cooking facilities, only a kettle and a toaster, so had to eat takeaways or Pot Noodles. I did try to boil an egg in the kettle, once. "Is that your hairdryer blowing the fuses?" Woody then asked. He would provide us with four pieces of bread, a knob of butter and a pint of milk for breakfast and we had a black and white TV in the room, two single beds and not much else. But Woody was okay with Lynn and me sharing a room and his partner, Pauline, was also fine about sheltering a lesbian couple.

One day there was a knock at the door and there stood Mum. "I can't believe you are living here… with that woman," she spat. "I want you to come home, right now."

That was the last thing I wanted to do, and I stood up to her. But when she came close to me I could feel that familiar fear rising in me. Her hand was raised and I expected to feel the thud of her fist on my face, but instead someone burst through the door and must have grabbed her hand. "You can leave!" Woody said to my mother, and she stormed out.

From that moment I knew Lynn and I had to move on.

It was about a week later that we found, very randomly, two double bedrooms in a large house in West Street, Burgess Hill. One of the other lodgers, Steve, was a guitarist known to me and he vouched for us being decent people. We took the rooms, after I had paid deposits for both rooms (I had just been paid for playing at a wedding), and we moved on from Woody's.

And who should be my first visitor? Auntie Daphne. "But Mum said you wanted nothing to do with me," I said, surprised yet delighted she had called round.

"Listen, Karen. It doesn't make any difference to me whether you're gay, straight, whatever, you're always welcome to visit us any time. You'll always be Karen to me." And then Auntie Gill's eldest son, my cousin Kevin, came to repair a window for me and he was just as kind: "You can never tell which direction your love will go," he told me. And he was right.

# DAD CALLING ME

BEING with Lynn was a blessing, at first. She supported me with my singing career and would come to gigs to help me clear up at the end of the night, but rather than being a couple we would have to pretend that she was my auntie. "Oh, yes, that's my auntie, come to be my roadie," I would say if anyone asked. It was not ideal, but it was necessary at that time.

Lynn was my rock. She showed me the kindness I so craved and she was loving towards me. She also introduced me to social drinking. And that was when things started to spiral out of control. I should have realised what was happening because every time I was with Lynn there was always alcohol around, and I had seen her drunk many times at the Butlin's hotel. Even back at Woody's, she had started to visit Jane down in Brighton and would come back really late, steaming drunk, or would miss the last bus or train all together, and she once got arrested and cautioned for shoplifting some drink from the local Tesco's store (which was embarrassing because my second cousin's husband was the manager).

It was no surprise really when she started to drink heavily when she was gigging with me. And, because she was my 'auntie', it was a green light to any single male to try and chat her up. The inebriated Lynn saw nothing wrong in flirting with these chancers while I was on stage and, of course, there was nothing I could do about it. It made me anxious. She was throwing all my efforts back in my face and I had no idea how to keep the lovely Lynn from turning aggressive.

It was inevitable that we started to fight about it. We really fought about it – literally. When I came to redecorate our rooms at West Street, I removed the sheet music from the wall (I thought it looked nicely decorative) and re-discovered the bloody evidence of our ugly quarrels – putting up music notation had been to hide the red smears from our violent clashes. And, it had usually been my blood which was drawn. If I ever tried to wake Lynn in 'sleeping it off mode' I paid for it; once she dug her finger nails so hard into my face it made tiny scars I can still see today. Drunk Lynn had no idea what she was capable of and as hard as I tried to get her to slow down her drinking there was nothing I could do. Her drinking was totally out of control.

I was infatuated with her – totally in love with her – yet she was being violent and claiming she no longer loved me; it was a pattern I was very used to with my dad. I could hear my mother in my head: "You've made your bed, now you've got to lie in it!" I felt there was no support structure for me to rely on when Lynn was far from me (family or friends) and the thought of battling to get gigs to keep the roof over our heads was exhausting just to contemplate. The fight had gone out of me. It was amazing how quickly my love for Lynn was turning into hate, when she was picking fights with me and she, as my emotional anchor, was no longer there. I felt so very lonely and lost.

I must have been at rock bottom when we left the pub in Wych Cross at 11pm that night in April 1985. After packing up my things, Lynn and I decided to drive down to Brighton to our favourite late-opening Greek restaurant in Preston Street. When we arrived, there were two men who Lynn decided she wanted to talk to and, of course, they thought this was an invitation to join us for our meal and they began to ply her with drinks. This was quite normal behaviour for Lynn and I was already so low that this pushed me near the edge. "Do you want to come back to our place?" one of the blokes asked Lynn at kicking out time.

"Yeah, sure," she slurred.

"Er, Lynn, I don't think so," I said, holding her arm. "Remember, we've got to be up early tomorrow."

"No we don't!" She shook my hand away and staggered out of the door.

I could not believe it. What had my life come to? Nothing. I was so disgusted with Lynn, with myself and I could see no way forward. Absolutely distraught, I got into Dad's car and drove straight to Beachy Head.

Did I mean to end it there, on the cliff in the dark? Yes. I was completely consumed with bitterness, hate and humiliation that I could see no other option than to throw myself into oblivion. It would be the easiest, and kindest, option to myself. And in the black sky I could see my father in true technicolour. He was holding his hands out to me and beckoning me forward. It was so tempting to follow him. I fundamentally trusted him and, without my mother around, we would get on so well. I would walk towards him. It was so easy. There was this magnet pulling me to the edge of the cliff. It was so tempting.

But there was also a torrential gale pushing me back, away from the edge. I was being pushed away, yet pulled too. Even if I turned my back on my father, the magnetic force was still there – it would be so easy. Yet the gale was pushing me in the darkness towards the silhouette of a phone box. All I suddenly had in my mind was, I must get to that phone box. Karen is talking now. Karen is trying to save Karen's life. But on the other hand, Karen is seeing her father and it would be so easy, so very easy, just to fall over the side of the cliff.

When I got to the phone box I hung on to it as though it were my long lost friend. It was the only friend I had in the whole world. The force was still trying to pull me towards Dad so I had to get inside it – the solid box would only ground me if I clung on. I picked up the receiver and shakily punched in 100 – the operator. I knew I had to call The Samaritans and I started to put my mearge collection of 10ps into the slot when Marion answered my plea.

"I'll phone you back," Marion told me, when I told her I had no more money.

"It's my boyfriend," I said, trying to control my sobs. "He's gone off with someone else and left me."

We talked about my boyfriend's drinking and the fights we had. I began to trust Marion.

"Actually, it's not a man. It's a woman," I admitted. I thought she might put the phone down on me, but I was pretty shocked when Marion kept talking to me.

"So where are you, Karen?"

"At Beachy Head. I'm being pulled over the edge and I really think I should go, but I wanted someone to know why I'm doing it, so that's why I'm talking to you, so that you know.

"I'm scared of doing it, but it's for the best as I can't live with all this shit – it will be a release. I just wanted you to know why."

"Okay," said Marion. "Do you feel unstable on your feet, Karen?"

"Yes."

"Then I want you to hold onto the phone box."

"I already am!" I had the phone in one hand and was gripping the door handle as hard as I could.

"Now, Karen, you keep holding on and I'm going to send my husband to come and get you."

"Would he mind coming out at this time of night?" I asked, suddenly concerned about putting this nice lady's husband out.

"No, he won't mind at all. He's going to come and get you. Now, what do you like to do with yourself in your spare time?"

We got talking about music and how I was gigging to pay the bills and that Lynn was throwing it all back in my face and how I did not have the energy to carry on and how desperate I had been to have a music career, and now it did not seem even remotely possible and how Dad had encouraged me with my guitar and how I wanted to join him now…

Through my tears, I noticed this elderly gentleman with glasses and grey hair, and this great big coat on, coming towards the phone box. He opened the door and grabbed hold of my arm. He took the receiver off me and said, "I have her now. We're on our way," and replaced it on the hook and he firmly guided me to my car. His car was in front of mine.

"Right, this is what we're going to do. You're going to put your hands on the steering wheel," and he physically put my hands on the steering wheel. "It's a fairly straight road and what you're going to do is you're going to follow my red taillights. Very slowly. I'm going to go and you're going to follow me and you're not going to deviate at all. Are you?"

"No." I was in an almost hypnotised state.

I calmly followed this man. I have my hands on the steering

wheel. They are locked on there. All I am looking at are the taillights of Marion's husband's car. I am not deviating. Just think about the red lights and hands on the wheel. That is all. And changing gear.

Eventually we got to Eastbourne. He took me into Marion's office, sat me down and left.

Marion and I sat talking until the birds started to sing. "But, Marion, what am I going to do?" I just could not come to terms with losing Lynn. Any normal person would have dumped her, but I could not even think about that. I was so attached to her; so attached to my mother substitute.

"I think it would be best if you could forgive Lynn," Marion concluded. I was happy with this. It seemed a good solution.

After leaving Marion, I drove to my mother's house. Despite my despair, perhaps because of it, I still wanted to see my mother and tell her that I had spent the night talking to a Samaritan. I still desperately wanted my mother to accept me, love me and perhaps by telling her I had come so close to jumping off Beachy Head she would suddenly realise what I meant to her.

"Oh, really?" was all she could say when I recounted my harrowing night. Nothing was ever said about that night again.

All I know is that Marion and her husband saved my life that night. I cannot thank them enough. My Spirit had a part to play, but the service the Samaritans and other volunteers provide up at Beachy Head is the reason I, and thousands of others, are still alive.

# ROLLING CAR

I might have forgiven Lynn, but that did not stop her from doing the same thing again. We had been gigging in Eastbourne and while I was on stage she was flirting with this bloke. It was the same thing every time.

It was so difficult to hold on to Marion's advice. Something in me was snapping and I could see the truth vividly. "You are pissed, and you're taking the piss. You have no respect for me," I thundered as I drove her back to Burgess Hill. We had to pass over Beachy Head and my head was filled with flashes of that night only a few months ago when I clung on to life. Lynn sat limply in the seat, too full of alcohol to raise any objection. I glared at her: she was supposedly my partner and I just did not know how to cope with her drunken antics.

I was speeding along, shouting at the almost lifeless body next to me. It was my turn to let it all out – and I did. I was so enraged that when the car hit the verge I hardly noticed and just turned the steering wheel harshly to counteract the slide. It was only when the car started rolling that my attention became fixed on the images which were playing slowly in my mind's eye. Like film exposures, they were shots from my past: my childhood in Cornwall, Lorraine, my father. All happy visions. I was so engrossed in these graceful, flickering images that I let go and relaxed. Just take me, I thought. I had already failed once at a suicide bid and I was waiting to die. Happy memories just before I die. What a wonderful way to go.

I barely even registered the car rolling three times. But when I came to, hanging from my seat belt, upside down, I was so pissed off. I was still alive. I had no bones broken. No cuts. No grazes, even. I had been absolutely convinced in my mind I was going to die and I was absolutely at peace with myself. I was not scared – I had surrendered my soul at that moment. That is why I was so bloody disappointed when I heard the emotional BANG in my mind and came out of my dream.

I looked over to Lynn, who was also hanging from her seat belt. "Are you alright?"

"Yes, I think so."

I knew we had to get out of the car because I could smell petrol and I had only filled up the tank that day, but I could not open the buckled door so I kicked out the remainder of the windscreen, undid my belt and fell onto my head. Having scrambled out onto the road, I turned to pull Lynn out and we scrambled away from Dad's mangled car and waited in the dark for someone to come. We did not have the luxury of a mobile phone.

An angel must have sent the next person who came by. He was a man with a beard, in a posh long car and I flagged him down.

"We've had a major accident," I said. "Could you call the Police and the Fire Brigade because I think the car's going to go up?"

"Yes," he said, and sped off.

Within minutes, the emergency services had arrived and luckily the car did not go up while we waited. The Police saw to Lynn's cut knee and called a tow truck for us. Nothing dramatic happened. Dad had always said that green cars were unlucky, but I had to disagree with him: his green car might have flipped multiple times, but we were miraculously unhurt. More's the pity.

I was breathalysed. Negative.

"We're not a taxi service," the young officer told me when I asked the Police to take my music equipment back to the Police Station with them. "But I will lose my livelihood. Please could you help me? Could you just deliver it and I'll get someone to pick it up?"

That 'someone' was Woody, our ex-landlord and my friend, who also came to collect us from the accident. He bought a flask of sweet tea.

"What am I going to do without a car?" I asked him the next morning.

"You buy a new one," he said.

"But I've got no money. It will be weeks until the insurance company pays out."

Woody lent me the £300 I needed and I bought a Mini that afternoon. Not only that, but Woody also put new brake pads on it for me and got me up and running. That very night, less than 24hrs after the accident, I was at the Wagon and Horses in Brighton doing a solo gig. My Spirit was strong now I had Woody supporting me.

"You've got to get back in the saddle, Karen," he had said, and having that push from him was all I needed.

My focus was now on trying to get international gigs. I had got back my determination and even things with Lynn were starting to calm down. My mind was racing again – another manic episode – and Lynn was not my sole focus. I started looking in *The Stage* newspaper for auditions to attend and I leapt at the chance of going to Manchester to get in front of Eva Clarence, the agent who I felt would be able to get me the big contacts abroad (she dealt with five-star hotels in the Middle East). Lynn came up with me in the Mini (masquerading, again, as my auntie) and I remember sitting in the dressing room, surrounded by agitated people, saying to her, "It looks as though it's going to be a tough one, but I'm going to go for it." The agents were hardly letting anyone sing a whole song.

But I confidently strode out on to the stage, knowing that I had pretty much mastered my act and how to play an audience. I sung *You Are The Sunshine Of My Life* by Stevie Wonder. I sung a country song. I sung *Three Times A Lady* by The Commodores. Beginning to end. Three songs. Unbelievable.

Eva Clarence said to me, "You show a lot of promise. You've got a very strong act. Where are your photos?"

"I've got these?" I said, offering her three snap shots.

"And where's your demo tape?"

I looked to the floor, embarrassed.

"What I want is a colour photograph, 8 x 10, glamorous. And a cassette tape. Then I can sell you. Do your hair. I don't like it brown. Go blonde. You've got a great body. You look good, but your hair's not right for the Middle East. We need blondes."

Lynn was thrilled. Mum less so. "I'm not giving you money just for any old whim," she barked, after hearing my plea for some help hiring a recording studio. It was down to me, so while I had spare time between gigging and drumming up business, I took on several cleaning jobs. It was exhausting, but for a few months I was fired up with the goal of getting myself sorted so I could be represented by an international agent, with a chance of hitting the big time.

In a funny way, I felt relieved because I knew that for Lynn and I to have a secure relationship I had to get these big contracts and provide for us both. For a while, even Mum came to some of my gigs and, at the end of the evening, Lynn would arrive at the table with two fat, short-stemmed glasses full of brandy and lemonade: "Here you are, Brenda. A little nightcap." A small truce, too.

But this brief respite failed to last.

# BRANDY AND LEMONADE

I knew each chemist shop could only sell me one pack of aspirins. I felt very naughty as I went from one shop to the next, convinced that the assistants would know what I was up to. But, of course, they had no idea. I had a plan and it involved 150 aspirins and a bottle of brandy and some lemonade – Mum and Lynn's favourite tipple.

It was a warm summery day, but the house felt cold when I went into my room; the one Lynn and I slept in together. I looked in the mirror and saw a different Karen to the one punters saw on the stage. This Karen had been told by her girlfriend that their relationship was over. This Karen had badly highlighted hair which needed re-doing, a spotty face and tired eyes. But behind this sad exterior was a focused 22-year old girl. I was focused on my plan and a voice in my head was keeping me strong.

I was not sad, in fact I was upbeat. I opened the packets of aspirin and laid out the 150 pills on my bed (I really hoped I had enough), then I got a pottery goblet from the kitchen and poured myself a large drink. I put on the 45 record of Kate Bush's *Wuthering Heights* and played it over and over again. I was convinced that Adrian would be able to hear it at top volume with my windows open wide. I was Cathy and Adrian, Heathcliff. Perhaps I was already dead? Would I come back to haunt Adrian?

While I started to feel sad about people I would never see again, like Lorraine, I was also excited about the prospect of once again seeing my dad who I thought would be sure to sort things out for me. I had thought about my short suicide note for four days and now I had to write it:

*"11th September 1985.*
*I can't go on in this world. I cannot see a clear way of being happy in my skin. In a world where I am shunned for being gay. I believe I am*

*not fit to live. I feel there is something wrong with me, but I don't know what it is. I am a bad human being, but I don't know where to turn for help.*

*I am confused. I have found love, but I cannot make sense of that love. Am I really loved? The foundations of my security are slipping away. I feel I have no support in this world and I cannot take the violence and pain any more.*

*My one true love, I lost, through no fault of my own. It is Adrian who I am thinking of today. This is not a cry for help – I really want to die.*

*Karen."*

I never mentioned in that note the fact that I was exhausted from working so hard, trying to get some financial security for Lynn and me and that that was still being thrown back in my face. Only the other day, she had gone off flirting. It was a vicious circle that I could not break, and now I was defeated. I had no useful qualifications; I had messed up my schooling. And Lynn was only a hindrance now, not a help.

The only person who could help me now was Adrian. He was my mental rock. I knew that, with his help, I could commit suicide. He gave me the strength I needed to get those little white pills down my throat.

And there he was, holding my hand. Dad had been there at the first attempt, beckoning me forward but I had not been strong enough to jump. But here was Adrian in my head, willing me on and, happily, I would now be able to pull it off.

I began taking handfuls of the tablets and stuffing them in my mouth, followed by a swig of brandy and lemonade. They got stuck in my throat so I took more drink. It became a frenzy of getting them down; several times retching and feeling sick. The goblet even started to foam from the backwash of chemicals in my mouth. But I was determined. The song played on – just like a band on a sinking ship.

I have no idea how long it took me to swallow the pills.

"Karen, what the hell have you done?" It was Steve, my neighbour. He had broken down my door and was now trying to drag me to his car. "I've got to get you to hospital."

"No, fucking way!" I tried to scream. He was ruining my plan. I felt sick as I staggered to his car, but I knew I had to keep the pills down. I had taken so many that surely I would be dead on arrival. Adrian was no longer holding my hand and this made me angry, plus the fact that Steve was not listening to my appeals: "The world's a fucking mess. Don't make me stay here, Steve." He kept on driving. I looked at the blue towel on my lap. Don't be sick. Don't be sick.

I was taken by wheelchair into A&E at Cuckfield Hospital where a female nurse seemed to think I had been there before and knew the drill for the stomach pumping. "I don't fucking want that – just leave me alone. I want to die. Just fucking leave me alone – it won't take long now."

I felt Steve's hands on my shoulders. "Please calm down, Karen."

But I did not want to be calm. I just wanted to leave this world.

I was not able to fight against the nurses as they put a pipe down my throat. I must have been going in and out of consciousness because I remember my knickers being taken off and a catheter being put into my private bits and a line put into my arm.

"The aspirins are in your blood stream..."

When I came to, repeatedly and briefly, I was aware of being alone because Steve had gone. It was all okay, though, because I was still going to die. 150 pills.

But I woke up.

I was put in a wheelchair and rushed to x-ray where, bizarrely, I met my mother and Sue. What the hell are they doing here? They were crying. I don't know what you're crying for. You didn't want me, I thought.

"What have you done, Karen?" asked Mum. "I can't believe it. They tell us you took 100 aspirins and have a 50% chance of survival."

Only 100?! I did not care to listen to her crocodile tears. I just wanted to go back to sleep, forever.

I slept.

I was woken again by the Sister in charge of intensive care shaking my foot. "Silly girl. Was it your mum, again?"

I could not answer. I recognised the lady as Jan Cross. I had played with her husband, Tony, in a band for a few years and I knew the family well, and she knew all about my mother.

"You better rest." I knew then that although I was in intensive care, I was going to survive.

During the night, the young male nurse (who I felt was gay) gently looked after me, changing my drip fluids and catheter bag several times. He also told me I had come on my period and that he had sorted me out.

In the morning, the consultant, Mr Hine, visited. "I was worried about you, Karen, when they called me last night. You are the biggest overdose we've ever seen at Cuckfield. You are very lucky to be alive. Now, if you'd taken that many paracetamol you would have been dead." I made a mental note of that fact for another day.

Mr Hine had apparently talked to my brother about my reasons for overdosing. "He told me you were in a gay relationship and that it was not normal. So, Karen, I put him straight. I told him, and your mother, that being gay is perfectly normal and that they have to lay off about you having a relationship with a woman otherwise the next time could be fatal.

"Do you know why you tried to commit suicide?" he continued. I regurgitated my suicide note. "What do you mean when you say you're 'a bad person'?" I was not up to telling him my life story. I was also not up to seeing my mother, who I could spy outside the ward. They respected my wishes and I saw her leave, in tears.

The next day I spoke to a psychiatrist from St Francis [the mental hospital] called Julia Sanders. I told her my story, ending with my confusion about not wanting my relationship with Lynn to end, but then also worrying about people knowing I was gay.

"So, what are you going to do next?" she asked me after I had told her about Lynn dumping me.

"I don't know. I certainly don't want to go to my mother's."

"If you think it might help, we can admit you to The Villa just while you get yourself sorted." The Villa was the admission's ward for the mentally ill.

I went up to The Villa the next day. I was feeling better. I knew I needed long-term help, but I did not really want to take medication. Perhaps I needed psychotherapy?

I left The Villa. I was not mad. Or bad. I had just suffered from a nasty case of PMT… so the medical experts told me.

And my sister, Sue, phoned me: "I don't mind you being gay, Karen. But you must never tell the girls [my nieces]." How very odd.

And I have never drunk out of a pottery goblet since, and probably never will.

# RUNNING AWAY

WHAT followed after that suicide attempt was nothing short of chaotic – an opportunity missed for the state of my mental health. An older, middle-class, lady social worker was assigned to my case. She was most unsuitable as, shortly after meeting, she revealed to me that she had never met a gay before and that I was her personal case study. She was just a nosy parker who was so naive; even more so than I. She was absolutely fascinated by me, and Lynn, and she tried to tell me that she saw no evidence of psychosis. Just PMT.

However, after several follow ups, Dr Ernest Brown, Consultant Psychotherapist, decided there was more to my 'emotional difficulties' than simply PMT. He wanted me to start one-to-one sessions with him, but I found it really difficult to express my feelings to him and I asked him to just prescribe me a regime, not involving medication, which would get rid of my fluctuating emotions. I just wanted to be calm in my mind.

Would this be achieved through his suggested membership of a small out-patients' therapy group? Or would it be better if Lynn and I went on holiday to Tunisia for a couple of weeks to get away from everything and try to rekindle our relationship? I turned my back on medical intervention and packed our bags for the sun – I was also responsible for the tickets and passports

Lynn started drinking heavily at Gatwick Airport. "The plane's going to crash, Karen, so I just need this to get me on board." I tried to reassure her and tease the drink from her hand, but by the time we were called to the departure gate I had to almost drag her there. I only briefly relaxed when we were seated in the aircraft, but as soon as the air hostess started serving drinks, I began to tense again. For the next two hours and fifty minutes I wondered if I had done the right thing taking this holiday. Lynn was loud when drunk and my stomach was in knots after making excuses for her unseemly behaviour on the flight.

But when I felt the sun on my face at Tunis airport I felt my father's presence and I held onto that feeling, knowing that he would protect me.

When we got to the hotel, Lynn stayed in our room 'sleeping it off'. I knew full well that I had to leave her alone, so I went out on to the beach, but was scared off by the attentions of the local men who thought I was rather attractive (I knew I was not) and thought I knew Princess Diana.

Actually, I did not have a moment's relaxation in Tunisia because even though I managed a camel ride and sunbathed, there were three of us on holiday – alcohol was the ever present interloper. I was becoming more and more frustrated with Lynn and I did something very silly when the man in the hotel gift shop became difficult with my drunken girlfriend who was getting close to breaking some valuable items. In retaliation, against him, against the situation and against Lynn, I kicked over all the stuffed camels which were lined up like soldiers along the shop floor. I left them both there – the argument having lost its heat – and walked off in a daze.

I headed for the beach, not noticing the hot sand burning my bare feet. I was chanting and talking aloud to Dad; he was with me, protecting me. I did not notice, at first, the Tunisian man who was following me. I was lost in thought and lost, quite literally, when I came to for a moment and realised I had walked out of the safety of the hotel beach area. The man came up behind me. He had mid-length black hair and mesmerisingly dark eyes. I guess he was around thirty years old. The man was handsome. He did not speak English, nor did I understand the local language.

I was simply dressed in a vivid, emerald green bikini and I did not realise how vulnerable I was. This hypnotist was looking straight into my empty soul and the water lapping around us made me surrender to him. My body became separated from my troubled, and uninhibited, mind. I could feel his strong arms around me and I was drawn in by the desire to be loved. We did not know each other's names, or anything about each other; it was to become the brief encounter of my life. Our connection lasted for moments in the Mediterranean Sea.

On the way back to the hotel, I felt like an accomplished heterosexual being – I had lost my virginity, finally. Part of me enjoyed the rebellion against the being I had become; against Lynn, perhaps. But I also felt scared and the emotional impact on my mental health would last the rest of my life. I said nothing.

Everybody was waiting patiently on the coach as the tour rep called for Lynn, for the third time, to peel herself away from the hotel bar. I was powerless. At last she moved and I followed her onto the coach to the sound of a slow handclap – to which Lynn replied, at the top of her voice: "Don't know what you're all making such a fucking fuss about; the plane is gonna crash anyway!" Gasps of disbelief and finger wagging followed us, as we travelled the entire length of the coach. I said nothing. I wanted to slip under the seat and hide, never to be seen again.

We arrived in one piece at Gatwick and, to my relief, made it back home. Never again, I thought.

I went back to my cleaning jobs, and gigging. My determination to become an international singer/guitarist, jetting off to the Middle East, had been reignited. I needed to get away from Lynn, and from everything for a while. Within the month, I had the demo tape, blonde hair and glamour photos. I was "Karen Young: Lead Vocalist/Rhythm Guitarist", ready for the big time. I could hold an audience merely with my voice, my guitar and a drum machine.

I was cleaning the loos in The Star pub in Haywards Heath one morning when I did the test. The window showed a blue cross within a matter of seconds. Oh my God, I'm pregnant. I am a woman, after all.

I remember going to Woody's house and telling him I was pregnant. "What on earth am I going to do?" I cried. I could not face telling my mother and hearing the lecture which would surely follow, and Lynn had told me she would leave me if I had the baby. Everything in my body was telling me to keep the child growing inside me, but how could I? Other doubts came into my mind: would I become violent towards a child, just like my parents, if I did keep the baby? Would it be safe with an alcoholic about?

"Well, Karen," said Woody, "There are such things as abortions."

"What's that?"

He gave me the phone number of a clinic in Dyke Road and I eventually found myself at Wistons Nursing Home for counselling.

This woman informed me that my 'embryo' was actually just a groups of cells and that I was not going to be losing a baby at all. I was just going to lose a few cells. "I'm not killing a baby, then?" I asked, for confirmation.

"No."

We talked about my financial situation. About my housing situation. About my relationship status. All the things which made me sure I did not actually want to have this baby inside me.

There was nothing positive mentioned about having a baby. There was nothing mentioned about the physical damage which might be caused during an abortion. Or about the emotional damage an abortion might cause long-term. Or about the fact that a foetus at eight to ten weeks is a perfectly formed little baby, with arms and legs and little feet, and even fingernails and toenails. I was never told these things; I had no idea. All I thought, when I signed the termination request form, was that I was killing off a group of cells. A bad egg inside myself. That was what Lynn had called it – a bad egg.

I had to wait until I was twelve weeks gone, and by that time I actually had a bump showing. Even my mother had noticed my 'weight gain'. "Are you sure you're not pregnant, Karen?" she had asked me at a charity fashion show we had been invited to.

"Oh, don't be ridiculous!" I said, "I'm gay remember." Oh God.


27th November 1985

I was put in a bed, covered only by a hospital gown and thigh-length woollen socks. I was so cold. Around me, there were other girls in their dormitory beds. Not a word was said. It was like an unwritten rule. Silence. You just looked at each other and smiled. I did not see anyone in tears.

My name was called and I was put in a wheelchair and wheeled into the lift and up to the operating room. I was anaesthetised and the next thing I knew was when I awoke in the recovery ward and told it was all over. I was taken back to the dormitory and not long after I was told to get up, get dressed and go and sit at the table (in the middle of the room) to eat some chicken soup and a bread roll.

All the girls sat. In silence. Nobody spoke. We just looked at each other, longing to talk about what had just happened to us, but not having the voice to do so. There was so much to say. It was the saddest table I have ever sat at.

Afterwards we were told to go downstairs to the waiting room. We waited. In silence.

Eventually, Lynn turned up. In a loud voice, she said: "Ay, ya naughty girl. You're coming home now." Luckily, when Lynn had dropped me off that morning, I had told the staff she was my auntie. That was that. We never spoke of it again. Never.

I got a cat called Emma not long after.

She got stuck up a tree and I called out the Fire Brigade – absolutely distraught, I was. I kept waking in the middle of the night, sweating and shouting, "Where's my baby? Where's my baby?"

And Lynn kept saying, "Emma's over there."

"Oh, good," I said.

# PREGNANT AGAIN

WITHIN a year, I found myself back at Winstons Nursing Home: the same silence, the same chicken soup and same table empty of conversation. I felt as though I had been carrying a boy this time because I felt different to the last pregnancy.

I named this baby, Sebastian. Lilly had been my girl.

Of course, Emma was my substitute for Lilly the first time round, although I never recognised this. It was Emma that actually led to this second pregnancy, in a roundabout way, because I had been in America gigging and Emma had not been looked after properly in my absence. She had had to poo in the pot plants and the house was absolutely filthy. Lynn had not kept her word. She had told me she would look after her while I was away.

I was so disappointed in Lynn – she could not be trusted with this cat, my baby. All she wanted to do was drink and the only person who was around to look after me was my old 'boyfriend', Henry. I would occasionally still work with him at the garden centre if I needed extra cash and after my second suicide attempt he tended to keep a close eye on me. When I came back from America, he was there, when Lynn was not.

It was the weirdest thing because normally I would never have let Henry anywhere near me (I never did, even when we were 'together') but one night, when Lynn and I had fought particularly badly, I left her to sleep off her drunken state, and I went to bed with him. It was the only time I ever, ever went with him and I fell pregnant. Why we did not use a condom, I have no idea. Did he want to get me pregnant? Was he just taking advantage of me when I was desperate? I should have been more aware of what was happening but, like my Tunisian brief encounter, my mind after a fight with Lynn was elsewhere. I was completely possessed by my emotions and not in control.

While I gave Henry the cold shoulder after I had slept with him, I was completely honest with Lynn. "It's Henry's," I said, after doing a pregnancy test. Part of me, again, wanted to keep the baby but I knew I was unstable and Lynn started going on about the 'bad egg' inside me.

"If you think I'm bringing that child up with you, you've got another thing coming," she said, dismissively. "You've got to get rid of it." I also worried about bringing a child into this hostile environment, and was by now worried about myself not being a fit mother.

I thought of the money I had had to scrimp together to afford the first abortion, and decided I had to face Henry. There was no other way that I could see. I visited him, unannounced, at the garden centre. I wondered who the bearded man was in the greenhouse, until I walked close enough to see it was a dishevelled Henry. He looked awful. "What's the beard about, you've never had one before?"

"Yeah."

"I've come to find you because I think I might be pregnant."

"Yeah. I thought you might be," he said. He was so subdued that at first I thought he really did not care. I had just told him I was carrying his baby and he could hardly bother to look at me.

Then he looked me in the eye: "Well, don't worry about it because we'll get married."

"But I can't marry you because I love Lynn," I said, shocked that he would even suggest it.

"Forget, Lynn. Forget her. We'll get married," his voice raised slightly.

"I can't because I don't love you."

"No, you think you don't love me. We'll have to get married."

"Yeah, but my mum will kill me if she finds out I'm pregnant."

"Don't worry about her. I'll talk to her. I'll sort her out."

"I will be killed, literally killed. I can't have it. I can't have this baby. And if you go and tell my mum, I promise you I'll cut your tongue out," I threatened. I was panicking now. "And Lynn will leave me – she said she's not having this baby with me."

"Forget her," Henry insisted. "Lynn's no good for you. Forget it all. We'll get married. We'll buy a house. We'll get married and we'll have that baby."

"I can't do it, Henry. I really can't."

His face still haunts me. He looked so depressed, so demoralised, and I just walked away. He followed me, "Look, I'll come by this evening and we'll talk about it further." But when he came round, I could not be moved. I did not love him – I loved (or was infatuated with) Lynn – and I was due to go to North Yemen to start a month's long residency in a hotel, booked by one of my agents, Charles Cassell. I was finally getting the international gigs I had craved, and Henry's pleas fell on deaf ears.

And Lynn, of course, had her say: "I can't believe it, Henry – you are a naughty boy! Getting Karen up the duff. You took advantage of her when she was feeling down and you think I'm going to have your child in this house?!"

Eventually, Henry agreed to hand deliver a letter to Mr Cassell in which I apologised for getting pregnant (Henry took the blame) and made it clear that I would have an abortion as quickly as I could, but asked if he could delay the Yemen contract for a few weeks. Charles was happy to do this, reported Henry on his return, and a story of delayed work permits was concocted.

Henry paid for the abortion and took me, without speaking, into the Nursing Home on 23 September 1986. When he came to pick me up he told me he had stayed in Brighton and had bumped into my mother and sister in Marks and Spencer's. He made up some cock and bull story about shopping for his mother's birthday present and told me how guilty he felt about lying to them. And I felt guilt about taking Henry's baby away from him.

During the silent car journey home, I felt bad that I was not going to marry him, that I did not fancy him, or love him. He was a kind, lovely person, the kindest person that you could ever meet, but he was not Adrian. And Adrian, who I had not seen for years, was the only man for me. If I could not have Adrian, I would be happy with Lynn. Blimey, I was so confused.

Lynn was full of chat when I got home, but I just went to bed. Emma curled up beside me and I decided to ask my nan to look after Emma while I was in North Yemen; Lynn could not be trusted with my baby.

# A MISSED OPPORTUNITY?

I really could not have moved to a more different world a few days after my second abortion. Here I was working six days a week, doing two 45-minute spots daily (at lunch and dinner) in a five-star hotel, being chased by a Saudi Arabian who said I reminded him (again) of Princess Diana.

"Can you sing me Jennifer Rush's *The Power of Love*, Karen?" he asked one lunchtime in the hotel's restaurant. I had only recently arrived in Sana'a, the capital of Yemen, and it was a difficult song to sing anyway, but when feeling sick with the change in altitude and after a bout of food poisoning, it was near impossible. "I am your lady, and you are my man," I sang. What subservient lyrics.

Saturday was my day off, which was the Arabic day of rest, so this good-looking Arab asked me out to dinner at the Sheraton Hotel which served alcohol (my hotel had none). That night, after taking my zinc tablet to calm my altitude sickness, I came down to the vast marble-sculpted reception to find Mohammed waiting. "My lady," he said, ushering me to the door, "pick a car." There was a line of Mercedes outside.

When he told me that he wore traditional dress at home, I just could not imagine this Western-dressed man in such attire. It made me giggle so much when I thought of him in a white robe, with a tea towel on his head. I enjoyed our meal, although I could not eat much, and when we came out after the meal I was surprised to see the same driver sitting waiting for us. "Why didn't you let this man go about his business and earn his living?" I asked Mohammed.

"I've hired him for the evening." I began to realise that things were done differently out in the Middle East. This was a far cry from my English life, of scrubbing people's floors and gigging to pay the bills.

The next day I was sitting by the swimming pool, as I had afternoons off, and Mohammed found me. He sat down beside me. "You should really get married, Karen, and stop doing these jobs out here."

"Well, I'm only 24," I replied.

He looked at me earnestly. "I would like to marry you and I need your brother's or your father's address."

"My father's not alive anymore," I said, flabbergasted.

"You have a brother?"

"Yes, I have a brother."

"I need his address then, please"

"But why do you need my brother's address?"

"Because I will fly over to England straightaway, First Class with British Airways, and go and ask your brother for your hand in marriage."

"But it doesn't work like that for me. We have to go out with people and if we go out with them for long enough and we feel confident enough and we fall in love, then we get married. It's simple." My heart broke at the memory of losing Adrian.

"Ah, but it doesn't work like that for me. We ask the man of the family and then we are permitted to marry the woman."

"Yes, but then you can take four wives [I knew that much] and I shouldn't be wanting to be one of four, really."

"Yes, but my brother and myself have decided that we would marry Western women, either American or English, and we would only take one wife each and that is what we decided."

"Yes, but how would I know that you'd stick with that? It's so different, the culture."

I did not feel any pressure from him, or nastiness, when I evaded the topic of marriage, which he bought up almost continuously. I was bombastic with him, but he never wavered. [I know my brother, David, would have loved the offer Saudi men give the head males for a bride's hand – I could just imagine it]. I did not tell him about Lynn, but maybe I should have as he would have dropped me like a stone, or had me stoned, perhaps. Instead, he bought me a genuine jambiya (ceremonial dagger), not a tourist piece of tat, from a back street market when I expressed an interest in buying one to take home. "You must wrap this carefully and put it in your suitcase, and not in your hand luggage, because it will be seen as a weapon," Mohammed advised. He also asked me to accompany him to breakfast with Ali Addallah Saleh, The President of North Yemen. "No, I shan't," I told him.

"But I want you to come. It will be very good for you to come."

"No, I shan't and I can't anyway because part of my contract says that I can't fraternise with guests and you're a guest. I can't afford to risk my work [as I knew from past experience]."

"But you don't need to work if you marry me. Look," he said, almost conspiratorially, "I own an oil well. Forget being a millionaire. Add some noughts. You'll never have to work again. I'll buy you a home in Belgravia."

"I don't even know where that is," I replied, stoutly, thinking it was a country I had never heard of. It was lucky that bolshy Karen was in North Yemen, otherwise I could easily have been lured because I was so naive.

Towards the end of my contract, the General Manager of the hotel invited me to his suite to discuss the extension of my terms. "I'm not sure I want to, really, because I've not been well since I've been in North Yemen and I think I should just return to England," I told him. He was the same as Mohammed, in that he kept going on. "We would love you to stay here, Karen…"

"No."

It was ridiculous really. Could these men not take no for an answer?

Then (I really should have seen it coming), this man tried to make an advance on me; his wife had been over from India just the previous week. "I've been watching you from my balcony when you sunbathe by the pool," he leered, "You have a lovely body."

Of course, I was not into married men at all, and I certainly was not into him.

I made my exit for the door of his apartment, but he pulled me back by my bra strap, at which I elbowed him and shut the door in his face. I went into my room and phoned my colleagues who played at the Sheraton Hotel. I was told to wedge a chair under my door handle as, being General Manager, the man would have a key to any room he wanted, and also to have a stiletto shoe by the bed. I found my pair of lethal four-inch-high, metal-heeled shoes – I was prepared to attack.

But underneath the anger and rebellion, I was also scared and upset. I felt I had no choice but to phone Mohammed's room.

"I'll come and get you," he told me. Later, in Mohammed's room, we talked about what had happened with the manager.

"Most girls working in the hotel would go along with his advances, because it would be bad for them if they had rejected him."

"But not an English woman – we won't put up with that nonsense," I replied.

"Yes, but imagine a little Indian girl that cleans the rooms. Would she reject him?"

I thought about one of my English clients trying it on with me when I was cleaning their house. No chance would I surrender.

"Well, any Indian girl with a mind of her own would reject him," I declared.

"Yes, but she wouldn't reject him because she'd lose her job."

"Well, I don't care about that. I'm not going to do things like that. Why should I?" I thundered.

I made up my mind that I was going to leave and I told the reception staff not to tell anybody about the arranged date and time, especially Mohammed. He had been very protective of me and honourable, but I really wanted to get home and be with Lynn again – the phone calls home were costing me a fortune.

Astonishingly, at five o'clock in the morning, Mohammed appeared in reception as my trunks were being loaded into the taxi. "What are you doing here?" I asked.

"I heard you were leaving." Money must have changed hands.

"I will come to the airport with you. You will come in the Mercedes with me and the truck can follow."

"No, no! If you're coming, then you shall come in the transport the hotel provides. You'll come in the truck." And so Mohammed got into the truck and we had a very bumpy ride. "God forsaken vehicle… you're such a British woman…" he moaned all the way to the airport.

When we got to the airport he had one last try. "Change your mind, Karen. Allow your equipment to go, but stay here and marry me. Or I'll come with you and ask your brother."

"No, No! I'm not doing that. I've told you. I do like you, but I don't love you. We don't do things like that in England!"

He swore at me. "I cannot believe you, Karen."

Even as we queued at passport control, he turned to me. "You, my lady, are making the biggest mistake of your life."

"Then I shall always have to live with it," I replied.

He threw his hands up in exasperation. He realised then that he was not going to get what he wanted, despite his wealth and connections.

The last thing he said to me was, "You're not queuing up with all this lot" and he said something in Arabic to the uniformed guards and one of them came and took me straight through passport control. I looked round at Mohammed and that was the last I saw of him. The guard took me straight to my seat on the aeroplane. I thought, just for a second, I could get used to this; beats my Cinderella days.

I did try to contact Mohammed again when, a few months later, I was working in Abu Dhabi. He never returned my calls. I had missed my chance. He had given me a one-day only offer.

Which was a shame because, by then, I would probably have accepted his proposal (although on reflection, it was probably a good thing I avoided life as a pampered Saudi wife – I am sure I have done more good remaining Karen Braysher).

# THE STREETS OF LONDON

COMING back home from North Yemen, after a month of being wined and dined and proposed to, was a shock. Much like coming home from Butlin's, I suppose.

I had a fight with Lynn about the state our rooms were in. It must have been a big one, because I seem to remember one of the other lodgers complaining to the landlord about me shouting and causing arguments. Then I got a letter telling me I was no longer welcome as a lodger at his premises. I had to leave.

I was bloody pissed off about that, but while Lynn stayed in Burgess Hill, I looked in the paper and found an advert for a bedsit in Keymer, near Hassocks. The lady owner wanted a 'single business woman'. That was me. She, in turn, was another one of the angels who walked into my life at just the right time.

My new landlady was called Pauline, but everyone knew her as Asphodel, and she was a lecturer in Religious Studies at Sussex University. She believed God was a woman; she was, quite obviously, a feminist. At first, because I was feeling so bad about my fractured relationship with Lynn, I took no interest in what was going on around me. I was safe, warm and had everything I needed at Asphodel's and that was all the attention I paid.

But my emotional state was further shattered by Lynn's sister, Jane, and one of her friends who visited me and warned me off seeing Lynn again. I was threatened with having my throat 'cut out with a scalpel' if I ever went near her sister again. They scared me off and Lynn kept away from me. I suppose we had had our last fight.

I am not sure how I was, emotionally, when I met Fay through an advert in *Time Out* magazine. She lived in Acton and I started to spend a lot of time with her, just going out with her and her friends and doing normal things. It was quite healing being around her. There was no alcohol, and my mother actually liked her. I suppose we had a relationship for about two years and even when we drifted apart all her friends picked up the pieces for a while and they took me out. I am still in contact with Fay; she was very good for me.

While I was with her, I lost my driving licence. It is a long story, but a bartender spiked my cocktail and I ended up marginally failing a breathalyser test. The case went to court, thanks to Asphodel telling me my AA membership included a legal service, and I was eventually given a quite lenient fine of £80 and had my licence taken away for a year (it would have been for longer but we pleaded special dispensation because I, as a musician, relied so heavily on my car). The bartender disappeared before the police got to him.

I sold the car for £300, which was the fine sorted, and I bought myself a pink push-bike, about three-quarters size (for my short legs), which I loved. I would never drink and drive again – not even one drink. I might not have had a car, but I could get around to my cleaning jobs and my loss of licence did not stop me. Manic Karen had returned.

Asphodel could not believe how I used my bike to get to jobs, even in towns far away. She could also not contain her excitement when I answered an advert for a 'front man', offering a month's contract in Iceland. The man who put the advert in, a bass player called Chris, came to see me at a gig in Brighton and offered me the job at the end of the evening. Fay and I then had to go up to London to agents in Dolphin Square and Carnaby Street to sign and counter-sign the contract. I dumped all my cleaning jobs and off I went without any hesitation. It was much less lonely being in a duet in these far-flung resorts and Chris and I worked well together. However, we only played four nights a week in the hotel restaurant and the rest of the time I was free to meet the locals and explore – which I did without Chris. He was more into the rock 'n' roll lifestyle, shall we say, and was quite content being in his room.

I had another angel in Iceland in the form of Mary, the hotel owner's wife, who took it upon herself to pay me my half of the contract in traveller's cheques so she guaranteed I got paid (the actual contract stated that Chris would pay me on return to the UK). And thankfully she did, because then I had an excuse for not giving Chris any cash to pay the UK agents – which he asked me to do on our return to Gatwick airport. Mary did not trust Chris and she put me on my guard and prevented me from handing over money which I am sure I would never have seen again. He swore at me, a lot, but bolshy Karen was adamant.

I decided I did not want to work with Chris again.

The *Evening Argus* provided the key to finding another musician I could duet with, and also who would become my gig driver (remember I had lost my UK licence). Keyboard player, Hugh replied to the advert in 1988; it was wonderful timing. We became 'The Karen Young Duo' and I also got offered another contact, this time as a soloist, in Trondheim, Norway.

I cannot begin to tell you how awful the Norway job turned out to be. The outbound plane made an emergency landing in a snowy field, I temporarily lost the acoustic guitar Hugh had lent me, my accommodation was miles from the hotel/pub and the hotel owners were arseholes. I felt completely out of my depth, and scared for my life. For the first time since childhood, I knelt down and prayed to God. I had to walk to work, in the dark, carrying my heavy equipment, along strange streets and I prayed for safe passage. I imagined my Dad on one side of me and Jesus on the other. Needless to say, I cut short my contract and returned to London with very little money. I went to see my agent in Dolphin Square, paid him what I owed, and when walking back to the Tube I noticed this old man playing an accordion in the street. There were no laws against busking, so when I asked the man if he knew of a pitch he pointed me in the direction of Hyde Park. "Someone got thrown off the pitch outside the Tube yesterday, for being useless, so if you hurry up you might be able to claim it."

The pitch was free, so I just put my guitar case out in front of me and started playing *The Streets of London*. Within minutes, people were surrounding me and throwing pound coins in. The station master told me I could stay, because I was very good – amazing. Even the Police were tipping their hats to me. I made £30 in one morning, enough to pay the rent for the week.

When I returned to Hassocks, I could not be bothered to start up my cleaning jobs again so I decided to return to the streets of London which seemed, to me, to be paved with gold. I went up very early every morning, without enough to cover my fare home, so that I was focused on earning. I gave myself targets. Manic Karen.

I dressed down, in fact so shabbily that a tramp once walked passed me and offered me a cooked chicken which he was holding secretly to his chest. After a while, I actually started to get worried about the amount of money I had on me and I seemed to be a magnet for tramps and homeless people and business women. Singing *The Streets of London* was like a hymn for displaced people, and the smart women were probably thinking, why is this woman doing this; putting herself in jeopardy? The song had four verses, and people would listen the whole way through. It made me money, that song. And it also gave me a chest infection from repeatedly singing it on cold mornings.

After a couple of weeks, I stopped busking but it taught me a great lesson: that in the flick of a switch anybody can be made homeless. The experience taught me humanity. When I later became a band leader at The Grand Hotel in Brighton, I used to end the night with a rendition of the song after saying, "Ladies and gentlemen, we are all going home to a nice, warm bed tonight. Please, may you spare a thought for those who are sleeping rough tonight on the streets and pavements of Great Britain." I never gave an explanation, but I sang that song with such conviction that people would always come up to me and ask me why I had sung that particular song.

# CHARITY CASE

BACK at Asphodel's, and recovering from my chest infection (at first a bout of bronchitis, which turned into pleurisy), I was beginning to struggle. It was inevitable after almost a year of mania, the depression would appear.

I needed money, so I started doing cleaning jobs again and I also started giving guitar lessons to children at the nearby special school. Hugh, who I did the occasional gig with, put in a good word for me and these children with social, emotional and behavioural difficulties would queue up outside my music room waiting for their lessons. I really understood those kids and loved teaching them.

But I had to ride everywhere on my bike, which was fine, but it was exhausting when my mood was so low. Part of me just wanted to sign on the dole and wallow in bed. Asphodel had also decided to sell the house, so I was now also facing the prospect of moving. As it turned out I did not have to go far as I found a room at an enormous house in the village of Hassocks. The owner, called John, was a schizophrenic elderly man, an old Etonian, who looked exactly like Captain Birdseye. He had a grand piano in the front room and played classical music very loud on his gramophone. He was ideal – a total eccentric and I grew very fond of him.

However, before I moved, it was totally the wrong time for me to have lunch with my mother and Sue. I should have known they would be far from sympathetic. "You're nothing but a waster," my mother started. "You've got nothing and you'll only ever have nothing." All this was said while she ate her salad. They were absolute shits to me that lunch time and I came back to Asphodel's and sat on my bed, sobbing. I believed everything they had said.

They were cruel, but they were right. As I sat there I thought of my present life and the trials of the past few years and everything hit home, especially that I was having to drift from one bedsit to another, and the fact that I had had two babies forcibly removed from me and the woman who had insisted this should happen was now nowhere to be found. I had been left without the family I had desperately wanted when I imagined a family life with Adrian, and my guilt at killing two souls was starting to seed. I did not even have my music to fall back on as I was taking a break from serious gigging, although I was learning classical guitar again and had passed Grade 3 with Honours.

I cried so much that afternoon that Asphodel heard my tears. "What on earth is wrong?" she said, sitting beside me.

"Well, my mum and Sue say I'm a waster."

I remember Asphodel handing me a tissue and saying, "This is ridiculous. Absolutely ridiculous. You are a such a strong woman. You don't realise, Karen, what I see. I see this wonderful woman going out on her bicycle doing cleaning jobs, pedalling for miles to earn money to pay her rent. That's what I see.

I see a woman running her own show and going out every Saturday night to do a gig with her partner. I hear a woman studying the classical guitar and I see children arriving by taxi for their guitar lessons. How can that woman be a waster?"

"Well, I'm a failure. I've got no qualifications. I'm a failure. I'm never going to be able to put a roof over my head. I'm a failure."

"No, you're not," she insisted. "What would you like to do? If I could wave a magic wand, what would you like to be? What can I do to help you?"

"I want my education," I said, wiping my eyes with the tissues. "I want to be a music teacher. I was expelled from school, it wasn't my fault, and it's not fair. I can't continue my career without qualifications."

Asphodel stood up. "But Karen, there are charities that will help you pay for that. Put your coat on right now."

I put my coat on.

"Get in the car."

"Where are we going?"

"The library."

The last time I had been in a library was with Mrs Stone ordering musical scores for my CSE Music. Now, Asphodel was helping me. "What did your dad do?" she asked, as she scoured this big book of charities.

"He was a bricklayer."

"Hmm… what about your grandfather?"

"A bricklayer, too, but he died before I was born."

"What about your mother?"

"Never worked…. Hang on a minute, my dad was a Freemason."

She snapped the book shut. "Brilliant – we don't need to be here. Let's go home."

"You can't read and write properly, can you?" she asked, as we sat at the kitchen table. There was no such thing as a computer with spell check in those days and I was trying to write a letter, but my spelling was so bad and I was getting muddled with the order of words. "Here, let me write it down and you can copy it." My heartfelt plea was written to my dad's friend, Albert, who was also a Mason. I hand delivered it.

The next thing I knew, Albert was on the phone. 'I didn't realise you were in such a poor way. I'll get help for you. Do not worry."

By the time I moved into John's house, which was within a week, Mr Rees, a Detective Superintendent in Sussex Police, based in Lewes, came to see me. "How long have you been living like this?" he asked, inspecting my holed shoes and scruffy clothes. I was a walking rag bag. Apart from my stage clothes which were pristine, I had nothing. After showing him my dad's death certificate, which I had a copy of, he said, "And why does your mother not help you financially?"

"Because of family difficulties," I said (Asphodel had already coached me not to open that particular can of worms if I was asked the question).

Following a further interview with Mr Rees, and with more help from Asphodel filling in application forms, I was offered a bursary of £18,000 which was a huge amount of money in those days, to be a music student at Chichester College to complete a Foundation Course (which was the equivalent of O-levels) and then go on to do A-levels. University would be next, to get a degree in music, and then I wanted to specialise in music therapy. So, I was looking at being at least 32/33 years old by the time I was qualified.

My niece, Karla, took me down to Chichester to look at student accommodation and all I could afford with my tiny accommodation budget was another bedsit. But I put down the deposit and moved in that September. But I just could not settle there. I lasted a week. I think it was the academic side which scared me off, and the thought of spending the next decade in education. Plus I was tired of living poorly, if I am honest. I had done my busking, scrubbed floors and lived in bedsits for long enough.

But I had another plan.

I moved back to John's and visited Mr Rees with two other career options which I felt were open to me (as they did not require any O-levels): hairdressing or floristry. Asphodel was furious because she felt I was wasting my musical talent and Mr Rees was not sure the Freemasons would accept my change of course because it was not academic enough. I was really tired by this point, and defeated. I had no fight left in me to try anymore – the dole queue was waiting.

But then, miraculously, Mr Rees came back to see me, after attending a meeting at one of the Grand Lodges in London. "We understand your position, Karen," he reported, "We want to help you. It's our duty to help you. We understand why you don't want to train to be a music teacher and you're right it would be a long haul and you're right that you have lived very, very poorly and not been looked after. Therefore the decision has been taken that we will back you to train as a hairdresser. However, you're not just going to be any old hairdresser. We want you to be the best. Therefore we are sending you to a private hairdressing school, and after that course you will go to a London finishing school to perfect your craft."

I could not believe my ears – I accepted within a heartbeat. I found a course in Brighton and, after visiting it, Mr Rees agreed my start date would be 1st February, 1989. He came to see me again. "You're going to be a hairdresser," he said.

"Yes, that's right."

"Well, would you kindly start looking like one," he said, looking at my scruffy clothes. He handed me a cheque for £500. "Go and buy yourself a new wardrobe."

"Really? I've never had that sort of money before." That conversation took me straight back to my young self, as a Saturday girl, being told not to return to the salon as I did not have a school uniform to wear. Now I finally had the opportunity to be smart and get on in the world, in a career which would set me up for life. I had my rent paid, a student salary and I just had to get on with it – my last chance to make something of my life.

There was a mix of people on my new intensive course, with different motivations for being there, but I was very, very focused on getting a roof over my head. I wanted to feel secure and getting my own place was crucial. I started off with no confidence in my hairdressing ability, because I still felt that everyone was better than me; I was still a bad person. But as I progressed I knew I was good and the course lasted less than a year so when I graduated with the basic qualification I was then off to London to Vidal Sassoon's to refine my skills.

[It was only on graduating from Brighton that the owner of the school told me she received a call every Friday afternoon from a mystery man called Mr Rees, who enquired about my attendance and my progress as a hairdresser.]

London was a revelation and within a few weeks I felt I was elevated to the next level. My music career (and personal life) had also been bubbling away during the year, so now there was no stopping me. Again.

# BEATS PER MINUTE

I suppose I was casting around for comfort when I first answered the advert in *Spare Rib*, the Feminist magazine which Asphodel had on her coffee table. "24 year old woman would like to meet another woman for friendship, lives between Crawley and Brighton, PO Box…"

The girl, Shirley, responded immediately to my letter in which I had mentioned I was a musician, by telling me she played keyboards. Brilliant, I thought, we should get on. I was just in the middle of moving to John's house so when I was settled in, I arranged to pick Shirley up from Hassocks Station (I had another car by now, bought from the local auction). And, oh my goodness, she was so attractive. When I took her back to my new lodgings, the other two male Australians who lived there could not believe their eyes. "Who's she?" they mouthed to me. They had no idea I was gay, by the way.

I had just started my hairdresser training in Brighton and Shirley was also a hairdresser, so we had plenty in common. She came to see me, and Hugh, play a gig in Brighton the following weekend, and her verdict was blunt. "You're never going to get anywhere with that duo. He's too boring." I suppose she had a point because Hugh was a magnificent piano player and musician, but it was certainly up to me to do all the entertaining.

"Okay, Shirley, it would be good to hear what you can do."

The following weekend she turned up with her keyboard and started to play. It was crap. My heart sank. "What about your voice? Can you sing, too?"

Shirley nodded.

But her singing was crap, too.

On the plus side, she was so attractive.

I thought long and hard about what I might be able to achieve with Shirley and I decided that I could make something out of her – talent, or no talent. I had found my next musical project. Mania stations, here we go.

We got our first gig, as 'Shady Ladies', through a friend of a friend, in a pub on Rye harbour. The landlord was only going to pay for a solo, so I thought I could bring Shirley on in the second half as a guest and get her to play a few chords on the guitar to accompany me on *Apache* by The Shadows and some rock 'n' roll number. She picked up the chords easily and on the night she came on the stage – this attractive girl playing a guitar – she was an instant success. I knew then that our duo would be brilliant.

The landlord paid both of us, and booked us for the following weekend. The hard work began. "Right, okay. We're going to practise more songs – you're a quick learner," I told Shirley. She went along with everything. She was such an upbeat person.

Our next gig was a Masonic event, not big, and I let Shirley loose on the keyboard and despite quite a few bum notes (a bit like Les Dawson), the organiser gave us a £10 tip. This was enough for me to go into top gear. "What we're going to do is we're going to go on holiday and get a sun tan," I told Shirley.

"Blimey."

"And then we're going to come back and I'm going to get Louise, my dressmaker, to make us some stage costumes and we're going to have some publicity shots done."

"Are we?"

"Yeah, absolutely."

I remember the day we had the photographs taken so well. We shook hands on the deal.

"I've got my name down for a council flat," Shirley told me when we first met. "But they tell me because I've got no children I might not get one."

"I want to get my own place, Shirley; we should aim higher than bedsits and council flats."

"But nobody in my family owns a property, not even my parents."

"Do you know what?" I asserted, "We can do better than that.

By the time we've finished in our duo, we'll both own properties."

Shirley had just laughed.

But now, posing for our photos with our tanned faces and sparkling costumes, I turned to her and took her hand. "We will both own properties, Shirley. I promise you. Shake on it."

"I agree, okay. But it will be a bloody miracle if it happens."

When I showed our photograph to agencies they were bowled over. "Who is this Shirley?" they asked.

"Oh, she's been to music college. She's brilliant. Don't worry about a thing."

Of course, I could sell coals to Newcastle when I was manic and had a goal – we were going to get a roof over each of our heads before we folded and that meant working incredibly hard, while we were young, and pretty, enough to do it. Even if we fell out and hated each other, we would carry on.

Every Sunday we would practise in Wivelsfield Village Hall and I basically square-bashed Shirley in how to look, how to stand, how to engage with the audience, how to play some bass guitar notes to support the drum machine and some tunes on the keyboard. There was no particular musical talent there, in Shirley, but I had a fantastic partner because in the end she had listened to my every word and she knew just what to do.

On stage we developed this rapport and banter. She was the tall common one, I was the short posh one, and we would argue on stage. We would accidentally drop something and show a little bit of suspender belt when we bent over. I suppose it was all part of covering up the fact that I had most of the musical talent and Shirley had the most sex appeal – we bridged the lack of musical ability by using some clever tricks.

By the end of 1989, on New Years' Eve at Moulsecoomb Social Club in Brighton, we had taken to wearing engagement rings on stage to stop us being mobbed by the crowd. It was such an exciting time as Shirley and I developed our act, and our relationship, plus I was by now a qualified hairdresser – a bloody good one.

The following year, we changed our name to 'Bouquet' and immediately got a contract in Abu Dhabi at the Holiday Inn.

It was during that contract we realised the potential of using technology to fudge Shirley's less than perfect keyboard skills. One of the other acts at the hotel was a duo from England and they had a Korg keyboard, the same as Shirley's, but they were using floppy discs to play backing tracks, while playing chords over the top to get a fuller sound. "We could do that," said Shirley, "then I'd never play a bad note again!"

When we came home, we both had hairdressing jobs during the week, but on Sundays I would help Shirley work out the notation (as she could not read music) and she would input the music using all the gadgetry available to us on the keyboard. It took ages to do, but between us we programmed songs as backing tracks. We added strings, bass and drums, and – hey, presto – we had the big band sound, with me playing live guitar over the top. It was phenomenal. It was cheating, completely, but everyone else was doing it, so why not us. It worried Shirley that people might see her inserting floppy discs and then floating her hands over the keyboards, but I had no such qualms. "Just lie," I instructed her. "Make out as if you're playing and if anybody asks what you're fiddling with, just say you're changing the battery."

If we were doing a dinner dance, Shirley would have several discs to change because we would go from slow music to get-up-and-dance music. While Shirley fiddled about, I just had to chat to the audience to keep their attention and when she was done, Shirley would announce, "Oh, don't she go on? How bleeding boring." And off we would go. I worked out that any song at roughly 120 beats a minute (as shown on Shirley's computer) would get people dancing (*I Will Survive*, Gloria Gaynor, for example), while songs at about 90 beats a minute (resting heart rate) or less were suitable for old-time dances and background music during dinner. I learnt to manipulate the dance floor using this simple principle and it worked; my dance floor was never empty. During an evening, the Korg ran out of several batteries!

We started to get bigger contracts, including a hugely successful stint at the Jordan InterContinental Hotel, playing one night in front of Crown Prince Hassan of Jordan, and our prices rose accordingly. We were looking at jobs of over £1,000 to play on New Years' Eve 1990 and often played for hefty amounts at HM

Broadmoor Hospital and Wentworth Golf Club.

I had also started doing some little acting jobs which had come via my agent. It was great to be able to say I was on *The Darling Buds of May*, *Doctor Who*, *Lovejoy*, *The Les Dennis Show* and *The Bill*. The girls that Shirley worked with in Crawley were beside themselves with excitement about what Shirley and I were up to, and would often come along to support us.

When I was manic (which I was for most of the seven years of 'Bouquet'), I was the complete entertainer, and that was one of the reasons we were so popular. There was one gig we did regularly, at the Burgess Hill British Legion, where they provided me with a table I could leap on (this was after I did it once) and from where I would play guitar, with a radio mike. I always thought the stage was too low at that venue so I shook things up a bit, and the audience then came to expect my antics. Other gigs would see me run the length of a row of tables using a long guitar lead, dodging drinks and nibbles, if I thought the audience needed waking up a bit. It became a bit of a trademark, so even when I did feel down, I still had to put on the professional smile and deliver the goods to meet expectations. Standing ovations were normal for us.

In the end, we both had to become self-employed so we could keep up with demand for gig bookings. Both of us became mobile hairdressers. I cannot list all the places we played at during our years together, but in 1994 Shirley and I eventually split when she put £48,000 into a house, down the road from her mother, and I put £10,000 down on a flat in Preston Park, Brighton, which was on the market for £49,000.

Shirley thought I had taken on too much mortgage, but I was adamant I could handle it after my accountant and financial advisor had finally been able to secure a deal (because as a self-employed, single woman it had been terrifically difficult to get any mortgage). It had taken several attempts to be accepted and it had been so hard to save with all my outgoings (Shirley lived with her mum so she had no rent or bills to pay).

[It was thanks to an inheritance from Nan (Nellie) that I could reach my target. She had died earlier that year and when she died, Lorraine and I lost our only positive female role model in the family. It was heartbreaking and I had to help Lorraine blow her nose all the way through the funeral. However, as a testament to Nan's kindness and goodness, Sir Peter Imbert (as he was then) gave a fond speech at her funeral as he had lived with Nellie as a child evacuee during the War. My dad always talked of 'Peter, the evacuee' whenever we saw him on the television or in the papers.]

With our properties bought, it was now time for Shirley to lay her cards on the table and she said, "I don't love you any more. I've got what I want and if you pay me back what you owe me, I'll say goodbye." At the very beginning of 'Bouquet', Shirley had bought all the equipment we needed so I paid her so I could keep everything (Lorraine lent me £2,000 as I had no money left after buying the flat). We shook hands, for the final time.

It was good to have a clean break because, by then, Shirley and I were not getting on at all. We were fine until 1993 when we invested in a new PA system, bought two new vans to transport all the equipment, talked about taking on another girl on saxophone to open up the act and take us further and we were playing festivals, corporate gigs, charity functions and massive Christmas parties. I suppose my behaviour started to disintegrate with the stress of the band, especially when we got a residency at The Grand Hotel in Brighton and I began to have trouble balancing the pleasure versus business aspect of our relationship. I was also holding down hairdressing clients, because that was going to be my bread-and-butter when the inevitable band split occurred.

We had fights (not as bad as the fights I had with Lynn, though) and these ugly feelings started to come back to me. I began to worry about myself. I had been stable for so long, and now I was starting to feel lost again. Shirley used to wind me up a lot (I thought on purpose), by being deliberately late or making mistakes. I was really annoyed by her behaviour, because I had made something of her, had I not? But, with hindsight, Shirley may have been driven to behave in such a way because of my erratic behaviour. When I got cross with her, she would tell me:

"You've got something inside your head that's not right. You're mad. You're not a normal human being. Are you sure you don't need to see a vicar and be exorcised?"

It was our agent's sister who first noticed something was wrong with me. Amazing that it should be a stranger who detected my imbalanced mental state. She met me at the Lakeside Country Club in Frimley Green where we were due to play and I was completely hyper, rushing around introducing myself to everyone, and getting furious with some man for making a compliment about my legs. "How dare you make that sexist remark," I had shouted in his face.

"What's wrong with you?" my agent asked. "My sister thinks you're on drugs, or something."

After the band split, my behaviour got so bad that when we had to do a few outstanding gigs and radio interviews our agent had to babysit us in the dressing room. Shirley and I could not stop fighting. We played on stage, then left separately. I can see now that I was ill again, but at the time I just thought I was a bad person. I had left that Karen behind for so long, and now here she was again.

Things did not get any better when I moved from John's house to my new flat. We both cried when I left as we had become friends – the odd couple. I would motivate him to cut the lawn, wash some of his clothes, make him something to eat and do some cleaning. He would proofread my letters and entertain me with tales of his schooling at Eton and gossip about the then Members of Parliament. I adored his eccentricity and, looking back, I possibly found some connection with him because of our mental health issues. He was such a nice man and I kept cutting his hair for many years until he died.

I was now living in this beautiful, brand-new, luxury flat in Brighton, but I was alone and unhappy.

# SAVED

AFTER Shirley and I had split, the depression was severe and uppermost in my mind was a tremendous guilt surrounding my abortions. I now so wanted children, but being bi-sexual was so confusing. Would I have a family naturally, or would I have to find a surrogate? Would I be able to have children in a lesbian relationship? It would have been so much easier if I could be either gay or straight, and then I would be able to narrow my options. As it was, I was just floundering about, getting nowhere with my biological clock ticking – I was nearly 32. This was 1994.

I became suicidal again. But this time around I did have some support in place. Patricia was a friend of Asphodel, and one of the loveliest people I knew. She had been giving me some healing, through hypnotherapy, and I was cutting her hair in return. It was she who told me something which turned my head against suicide. "When you commit suicide the spirit world will send you straight back. Why would you want to come back and go through all your life again?" It stopped me in my tracks. Fuck that, I thought.

I continued with the hypnotherapy and, although not believing in it all, I did begin to feel slightly better. I do not know if it was the healing music, the incense, the low lights, the relaxed state or her suggestion to 'let Shirley go and send her love and light' that did the trick, but I was always able to sleep after her sessions.

However, in the end I went to the doctors and was diagnosed with clinical depression and referred for counselling. I was put on the waiting list… but was never seen.

With Shirley 'released' from my life, I turned, again, to the personal ads. I was useless at being on my own and really wanted to share my life with someone. This time it was Pam who caught my eye, but her story, I was to find out, was almost as crazy as mine. She was married, with two children (who, incidentally, would have been the same age as Lilly and Sebastian), lived 50 miles from me and was 11 years my senior. She worked in the police as a civilian, was a parcel courier and also worked in a bar. Her husband was a builder and they had been to marriage counselling after she had had a breakdown. The counsellor had said to her, "If you're gay then you must find a girlfriend." Her husband was quite happy for her to go and have other relationships, and he was living in a caravan in the garden while she was in their house – it was cheaper than divorce. Weird, though.

At first it was fine, because I was the pop star from Brighton (in Pam's children's eyes) and they all loved coming to stay for weekends in the posh flat in town. I had an instant family and, my goodness, I needed that. Pam and her children filled the gaping hole in my life.

They used to come and see me play gigs. I was now working with another girl and I renamed the band 'Karen's Bouquet'. There was a succession of other girls in the duo, each of whom I trained up. They could mime to a dummy keyboard really well and, unlike Shirley, they could sing and do harmonies, so it brought a bigger sound and that made my life easier. Technically it was a better duo, but there was never that same chemistry between us and, even if the audience did not notice, I certainly felt that on the stage. It did not stop us getting plenty of work, though, and what with my mobile hairdressing as well, I was raking it in. The band actually lasted for another seven years, and during that time it got bigger and I had saxophonists and all sorts playing for me.

In contrast to this great career, my personal life was not quite going to plan. As time passed, Pam and I became more serious and I wanted her and the children to move in with me – buy a house together. But she just could not see how that might happen. Her stumbling block was her beautiful house and lifestyle; she was reluctant to leave 'home' and lose everything. I was not enough for her. She had already asked me to dress more butch, cut my hair and lose weight (which I did and almost became anorexic), but she was always wanting more. I was so heavily influenced by this new mother figure (because I can now see what these older women were), who was shaping up to be as disappointing as Lynn had been. Inevitably, we started to argue and things went downhill.

I was doing some soul-searching, again. It was difficult being the 'bit on the side' in a marriage as I had to fit into Pam and the children's lives, which meant I spent a lot of time on my own, and I was beginning to realise that my dream of our being a family was not going to work out. Pam was just as unstable as me and we were definitely not on the same path in life. She used to say to me, "This being gay is such a new thing for me, I feel like a teenager. I want to go out with different women."

"But I'm stable, Pam. Good career, own home. How are you going to find that again?"

"I'm not sure I want all that, Karen. I want to be free to explore."

About the same time as I was losing Pam, and my mind (again), there were a couple of good things in my life. Firstly, I managed to get my NVQ Level 3 Advanced City and Guilds in Hairdressing. I went one evening a week for a year.

I also had Patricia still in my life and she was encouraging me to explore the spiritual side of my personality. "But I had an experience when I was a Redcoat which scared me," I told her when she suggested we should go to the Spiritualist Church in Hove. "I'll never go again!"

But she persuaded me, telling me that my father might have something positive to tell me; just when I needed him most.

And Dad did come through for me, and Patricia was right there to support me. The medium leading the readings came to me. "I have a ladder and I have books all around. I see you studying." Well, I was studying because I was doing my hairdressing course. "And I see someone here who is cleverer than people actually think; a person who is a Master, but has no evidence of being a Master." If you unpacked that, it was right. I had left school with no qualifications, but I was intelligent and had made something of my life. The medium continued: "Your father was a builder; his name was Reg and he died of a heart attack." The message to me that day was: continue to study – which I did.

In the back of my mind I had been thinking about the ending of my musical career and it worried me that with a mortgage to pay I would be relying on my hairdressing for my sole source of income. What if I had an accident and broke my hands? With Dad's message running through my head, after my hairdressing course, I decided to take adult education classes in social psychology and I followed that with an adult and further education teaching certificate; I would then be able to teach adults anything I knew about or was qualified in. It was my insurance policy. It was also a huge step for me as I had always struggled academically, yet Dad's message about studying spurred me on and the teacher training course I found was mainly practical-based, with moderate paperwork. If Dad was by my side then I would be okay.

Teacher training also opened up my world in another way. During one of the brainstorming sessions I had been asked to write the resulting ideas on the white board, but because it was a stressful situation I had a blank mind when it came to spelling. I could not even spell 'cat'. It was so embarrassing, but after the class my teacher, an older lady called Eve, said it would be a good idea if I went to learning support to take a dyslexia test.

"How would you feel about that?" she asked. "Would you go and do that for me? Just make an appointment."

"I've heard of dyslexia, but no one has ever mentioned that I might have it," I told her. "But I've never been able to spell, and my words get jumbled all the time, so I'll give it a go."

The test was conclusive – at 35 years old (this was 1997), I was eventually diagnosed with severe visual dyslexia. I nearly kissed the man who told me. It was such a relief to know that I was not stupid, after all; it was no wonder I could not write properly and had struggled with English and writing essays. I was also furious that I had gone through all that trouble at school, causing disruption in classes rather than be seen as stupid, and getting poor results and no one had picked up on it. No one had taken me to one side and seen this as the problem; instead they had focused on my bad behaviour.

"It's a familiar tale," the tutor told me. "Dyslexia was never recognised when you were at school. So many people were just labelled as stupid, and their school years were a disaster."

I immediately bought some books on dyslexia and everything slotted into place. I came to realise dyslexia was actually a gift because dyslexics have very good spatial awareness and the professions with the largest percentage of dyslexics are hairdressers and draftsmen; seeing the finished product; seeing shapes; estimating measurements by eye. I see the positive in being dyslexic, I really do.

I would like to be able to tell you that my bipolar was also diagnosed that year, but it would take a lot longer. The year before (1996), when I had just turned 34, I received my first diagnosis of clinical depression from my new doctor in Brighton. I had been to see Dr Lewis out of desperation as my hypnotherapy sessions with Patricia had failed to find an answer to my heart-breaking dilemma of what to do about my married girlfriend – 'the higher self of Karen will find a way to solve these problems' messages had not worked. I was in a mess.

After hearing about my feeling depressed for 10 years (on and off), my poor sleep, reduced appetite, weight loss, suicidal thoughts and constant tears, Dr Lewis prescribed me Fluoxetine (Prozac), 20 msg daily, and sent me to see a counsellor.

Mrs Suzanna Lobb was excellent. I had numerous sessions with her and we talked about my problems, my feelings and my past. She was someone I could trust and I felt safe talking to her. We talked about my confused sexuality, switching sexuality when Dad died, Mum throwing me out of the house 10 years earlier because I was a lesbian, guilt over the abortions and being excluded from school. We then started to unpack my childhood... and it was a revelation.

In answer to my conclusion that everyone got hit as a child, she said, "No, Karen. I see I'm going to have to teach you that children are not for punching. You were not just smacked, you were hit. You're not a punch bag."

"But my mum and Sue always told me that I deserved it all."

"I don't care what they told you. Children should not be hit."

I had always felt, up until that point, that the beatings were normal, part of family life and done because I was a bad person. I deserved those punches and kicks to my head – I was out of control and violence was the only way to deal with it, and me.

But Suzanna Lobb made me see differently. She recommended buying a book called *Toxic Parents: Overcoming Their Hurtful Legacy and Reclaiming Your Life* by Susan Forward. I devoured that book. I cannot tell you how much I connected with it: I was reading about myself. I could not believe it. I talked to Patricia about what I had read and she suggested reading Alice Miller's work. Alice Miller was a German psychologist who wrote about child abuse/mistreatment and its lasting effect. I could not get enough of these books because I was reading about me and the abuse I had suffered as a child and how this violence had affected all my relationships.

I was so angry with my parents, especially with my mother – and that is why I began to see my father as the instrument of my mother's hatred, the bullet in my mother's gun.

It was Mrs Lobb who opened my eyes, and it is thanks to her that I can talk about the abuse I suffered without tears or emotion.

During one session, I went into a sort of trance when I was talking about being kicked and Mrs Lobb asked me, "Where are you, Karen?"

"I'm out of my body. It's too painful, so I have removed myself."

"That's a known coping strategy, Karen," she told me when I came back to consciousness, "that children use when they are being attacked with violence."

Even today I can still remove myself when I feel pain – like when I am at the hygienist; I can actually fall asleep.

Then Mrs Lobb asked me how I was, spiritually. "What do you mean, spiritually?" I asked.

"What faith have you?"

With my recent forays to the Spiritualist Church and my meeting with Dad, I said, "I'm a spiritualist." And that was the first time I defined my chosen 'philosophy'.

# BABIES

DESPITE continued counselling, though, and the Fluoxetine, I was still suffering. I no longer had full blown depression, but everything was blunted. With Pam now out of the picture and a brief fling with Woody, the landlord, over (I feared I might get pregnant), I became friends with Pat. This lady was from Eastbourne and had horses, and four children, including twins who were roughly the same age as Lilly and Sebastian. Going out with her into the great big outdoors at weekends was the best thing for me and I was able to leave my flat for the fresh air and exercise. I came off the Prozac.

But, despite my previous concerns of falling pregnant with Woody, my desire to have children started to take over my life. It was an urge which I could not control and, with Lilly and Sebastian lost to me, I was desperate to have more, but was I truly gay, and, if I was, would I feel comfortable with lesbian motherhood?

After much thought, I decided IVF would be my best chance of motherhood and Pat provided me with so much support when I decided to put an advert onto a website which married up gay men and women to become parents. Barry got in touch. He was middle-aged, working in local government, did not have a partner, was financially stable and was desperate to have a child, too. Pat and I met up with him and we decided he would make a nice enough father, so Barry and I went to the Churchill Clinic in London to be checked over. This was in October 1997 (just after my being diagnosed with dyslexia).

It turned out that Barry's sperm count was fairly normal for a man of his age. It was me who was the problem. My heavy periods (and bad PMT) should really have been a warning sign because it turned out, after scans, laparoscopy and hysteroscopy, that I had fibroids and scar tissue from the abortions. There was also endometritis and a perforation to my uterus. After treatment, the consultant removed scar tissue which, when gathered together, resembled the size of a football – there would have been no way I would have got pregnant with Woody, or with anyone else, naturally.

Then came the turkey baster. Every time I ovulated, I would ring Barry and he would dash down from North London, produce his sperm and I would do the basting, with Pat's help. The reality of having a child with Barry was a concrete possibility now, and I had to try and get my head around being a lesbian mother. We tried the less than attractive procedure countless times. Nothing.

Of course, my depression came back after trying unsuccessfully. Not only had I started to question the wisdom of what I was doing, I was also beginning to doubt Pat's commitment as she was so tied up with her own children and horses and I could no longer visualise parenting with a man who lived so far away in London. I was also beginning to doubt my ability to be a mother, too. What if I turned violent, like my parents had? Would I be able to cope as a single parent? And, then, there was my mother's comments: "What are we going to call this baby?" she asked, "A test tube baby?"

I suppose I was trying to find an excuse to call a halt to basting when I asked Pat to come with me to visit Barry. I was starting to feel a bit uncomfortable about him as we knew nothing really about his background. Instead of meeting at his house, we were invited for a meal at his friend's house. They seemed perfectly nice and normal, but there was still something niggling me. If I had a girl, would I really want him to look after her for a weekend? I went up to London a week later, on my own, as I had arranged to see his home. And I am glad I did.

The house was totally creepy – like an elderly person's house. Whilst it is one thing to go to your nan's house to be faced with cupboards full of blue glass trinkets, it does ring slight warning bells when a man in his 40s chooses the same interior design. It was hard to put my finger on what was wrong – it was just that something felt off. Call it women's intuition. I came home and thought long and hard about whether I was just depressed because I was not getting pregnant or whether there really was a concern about Barry – beyond his appalling taste in ornaments.

I wrote him a letter. I was becoming emotionally disturbed by the failures. We had tried and tried but nothing was happening; I did not think I could carry on. Barry was lovely about it and said that he respected my decision and was glad he was able to pay for my scans and operations. I thanked him.

I went back on Prozac.

Mania set in and my brain started working out an alternative plan. What about I do artificial insemination with an unknown donor and I take on the responsibility of a child by myself? Maybe I could become a student at the university and become a lawyer? With my dyslexia now diagnosed, I felt perfectly able to do such a degree and I knew that I could argue well. I would specialise in litigation involving hair disasters – combining hairdressing and law. It would be a perfect career for motherhood as it would pay the bills and there was a creche at the university.

So, I enrolled on an access course at Brighton College two mornings a week, as I did not have O-levels, and I found it impossible. I had to do Maths. I was confused and I just could not cope with it. And that was the end of my law career. But that was not a problem, I could just keep earning good money from my mobile hairdressing and get on with the IVF and get my baby. The NHS had agreed to fund two cycles of IVF in March 1998.

However, IVF scared me – all those drugs and the possibility of multiple pregnancies. I began to doubt my ability as a mother again and it was around this time that I became convinced that I was not a proper lesbian and neither was I bisexual. My sexuality was so obviously the root cause of my depression during these years and I found myself trying to blame everyone and everything for my change in sexuality. It had been brought on after my dad died and I wondered, at first, if it might have been my grief which had thrown me into the arms of Lynn – at 13 years older than me, very much the mother figure I craved. Perhaps my line of relationships with woman was just my searching for that mother figure, which would explain why I felt so abandoned when things started to go wrong with each of them. And violence was my natural mode when angry; I had learnt from childhood abuse to lash out.

Could the childhood abuse have turned me into a lesbian?

Then I began to wonder if the drugs my mother had been given when she was in early pregnancy with me were the cause of my sexuality – I remembered Dad saying he took her out of hospital when he realised she was being given another anti-sickness drug.

I decided against IVF, but I was still absolutely desperate for a baby.

In 2000, I started to see a consultant at The Esperance Clinic in Eastbourne, who puts me on Clomid to help me ovulate. Clomid and Prozac. Prozac and Clomid.

What sperm donor should I choose? I would like a tall man, of Scandinavian descent, as they will cancel out my shortness and Scandinavians are quite intelligent and they are quite stable; cancel out my mental health issues. And they are fairly muscular, the men, and they are tall…

It was like ordering a bottle of wine, because when I ovulated I rushed down to the clinic, on my own, and chose my semen. "Is this alright, Karen?" the nurse said, showing me the syringe. It cost £300 for one treatment. It was the weirdest, most uncomfortable moment, because I was all on my own, no one there to support me. I remember thinking that if this did not work then I would not try again.

It did not work.

Something in me broke. I sat in the doctor's surgery in floods of tears. "What else can I do?" I sobbed. I was at the end of the road, with no baby in sight. I had been defeated and it was the worst feeling in the world. Pat went out and bought me another cat – Bertie – and I cried with joy.

Bertie had a habit of jumping on my bed early in the morning and usually I would turn over and fall back asleep, but that morning I got up in the dark to make a cup of tea. After I had fed Bertie, I flicked through the copy of the *Evening Argus*, which for some reason I had bought the day before, and when I came to the property pages a house just flew out of the page at me. I phoned the estate agent straight away and got the answer machine, of course, because it was so early in the morning. "I'd like to arrange a viewing as soon as possible and I'd also like you to come and value my flat."

Amazingly, my flat had doubled in price so when I met the owner of the house in Falmer, I found myself shaking hands with him and saying, "Don't sell it to anybody else, because I'm going to buy it."

And I did; within three months I had moved in. I lived on my own and because I had finally retired from gigging, just shy of 40 years old, I took in a lodger to help pay the bills and also provide some company. I knew full well that I was no good on my own.

I also made a vow not to have another relationship. I had been hurt enough and now it was time for me to regain some self-confidence, emotional independence and create a home in which I could feel comfortable. Unfortunately, in time, I did get another girlfriend, called Alison, but, in my defence, she did sort of wheedle her way into my life. She was 11 years younger than me (perhaps a role reversal had occurred and I was now the mother figure) and we spent eight years together. It is a rather long, and uninteresting, story with Alison, but we met through spiritualism and it started with her pushing out my lodger, continued with her drug addiction and ended in violence. Same old story.

PART II    COPING

# BIPOLAR DIAGNOSIS

I want to end my story on a hopeful note, so I want to tell you how I finally found some peace in my life.

Whilst I was diagnosed with clinical depression in 1996, and had been taking Prozac on and off for a decade, it was not until I watched Stephen Fry's documentary *The Secret Life of the Manic Depressive* in 2006 that a light bulb went off in my head. I had obviously never approached the doctor when I was going through a 'good mood' period and that is usually why it takes the mentally ill so long to get a diagnosis of bipolar – because you never go to the doctors when you are happy.

I sat watching the first part of that film, thinking bloody hell, this is weird. At the time I was having problems trying to build a studio flat extension to house a student lodger, and Alison and the neighbours were making life difficult for me. My suicidal thoughts were beginning to bubble again but even though I was planning my funeral, I could still relate to Stephen's manic periods. I rang Pat – as we were still good friends – and I asked her, "Pat, do you think I'm a bit manic?"

"Yeah, of course, you are!" she replied, without hesitation.

It seemed that even my doctor, Dr Lamb, had had an inkling about me because when I went to see her and told her about my possible solution to my almost life-long emotional instability, she said, "There are two people in my practice that I have had my worries about with bipolar and you're one of them." She gave me a mental health questionnaire to fill in, which indicated I was depressed, then referred me to a psychiatrist at the Mental Health department of Brighton General Hospital.

After an hour's whistle-stop tour of my life, the consultant asked me to come back the following week. "You have bipolar 2 disorder, Karen," he told me, at the next meeting. "This means that your elevated moods are less intense than full blown mania (they are known as hypomania), and you suffer more often with episodes of depression, than people with bipolar 1.

"The chances are that you've always had it, at least for a very long time. No matter how much counselling and other therapies you may have had, they would never have touched this condition. You have a chemical imbalance in your brain and it needs to be addressed by medication."

I cannot tell you how relieved I felt. Finally, at 44 years old, I knew what was wrong with me. I was not a bad person; I was not a worthless person; I was just … mad, but treatable.

And so began a long journey, with Dr Dingelstad, to find the right medications for me, because some of them (like Quetiapine – an antipsychotic) made me unable to get out of bed in the morning as I felt like I had been hit over the head with a sledge hammer. Some days I would have to pull over in the car to sleep in a lay-by. Another drug made me have involuntary mouth movements which made a funny noise, and yet another caused hair loss and there was no way I could continue on that, being a hairdresser. Despite a cocktail of ever-changing drugs, the search for the right medication took about a year and a half and I even visited the Bipolar UK Conference in London to try and find the answer.

Eventually, one of my hairdressing clients suggested I try Carbamazepine (an anti-convulsant for epilepsy) and that seemed to ring bells because there was a history of epilepsy on Dad's side of the family. Dr Dingelstad put me on 600mg of this drug, along with the Prozac for the depression, and Dr Lamb prescribed Thyroxine to treat my underactive thyroid and statins to help reduce my raised cholesterol (precautionary because of Dad's heart attack). But my depression was not really lifting, so I went from Prozac to Venlafaxine (a modern anti-depressant).

This mix worked well until I started to put on weight, due to the Carbamazepine, and Alison started belly aching about it. I tell this next story, because I want to show that even though a diagnosis of bipolar has made my life much better, and easier, there are some occasions when things can go wrong.

After talking to Dr Dingelstad, and to please Alison, I decided to come off the Carbamazepine to give myself a chance to lose some weight. But then the burger man took up his residence near our house. He was just parked up in the neighbour's garden, without planning permission, selling burgers to all the football supporters coming in by train to the new stadium nearby. As far as I could see he was taking hundreds of pounds every time he started frying, but it was like living next door to a fairground because the smell was so awful.

I had become obsessed by this bloody burger van. The previous year, I had had the Council in, Health and Safety and Environmental Health checking for rats and monitoring smells, but no one could get him moved. He went away out of season, but was back in August 2014, ready for the first football match.

We had returned from a shopping trip to find the burger van belching out its obnoxious fumes and Alison went out to confront the man, while I took in some of the shopping bags. I was also angry to see the van back, but I was more focused, at that point, on getting the frozen food in the freezer. As I came back out to the car for more bags, I saw Alison start to wave her arms about and shout at the man and two of his colleagues. Something in my brain snapped. I saw red, thinking he was going to hit her. I was already wound up because I was without my mood stabiliser, but what happened next I cannot really explain, because I lost control – much like my father used to do.

I ran out of our garden gate and literally picked up this guy, who was a little taller than me, by the scruff of the neck and lifted him off the ground. I was so incensed I did not even know my own strength and I shocked him, as well as myself.

"I don't like you. Leave," I said, and dropped him. He crumpled to the floor at my feet.

Next I turned on his colleague, a very tall man who was talking on his mobile phone and I kicked it out of his hand. I jumped up as high as I could and punched him on the side of his face. Finally, I got hold of his mate's big beer belly using the palms of my hands, squeezed hard, and I said, "And you're ugly, too." I pushed him away, turned on my heels and, as I walked back to the house, I turned to see them all absolutely gobsmacked. "And you're all ugly!" I shouted. I think those words upset them more than any other action I had taken.

That is what coming off the anti-mania medication did to me. I was so hyped up but I still went to the car, got the last of the shopping and went back into the kitchen. Alison ran upstairs in tears. I continued to put away my shopping. Within what seemed like minutes – I could not believe it – the police called round and I calmly opened the door to them.

"We've come here, Miss Braysher," began one policeman, "because we've had reports that… you… have assaulted some men." I sensed that, as he was looking me up and down, he could not quite believe that little old me could have done such a violent thing.

I surprised him. "Well, I suppose that may have happened, officer," I said.

"Well, I'm sorry, but in that case," he continued, almost regretfully, "I shall have no other option but to ask you to accompany us to the station."

"Okay, fine. But can I finish putting the shopping away first?" I smiled, innocently. "I'll make you a cup of tea while you wait." Amazingly, they agreed to my suggestion.

With the shopping bags emptied, and their tea drunk, I then called up the stairs to Alison. "I'm just popping down to the police station for a while; the police want to have a chat with me."

"What do you mean?" she said, coming down.

"They've sort of arrested me."

Alison became quite hysterical.

I was put in the car and when we got to the station I looked up at the policewoman on the tall desk and replied to her questioning. "Are you on any medication?"

"Yes," and I gave her the list.

"Do you have any illness?"

"Bipolar."

"We will get you an appropriate adult."

"And I would like a duty solicitor, please," I added.

I was locked in a cell and I waited. And I waited and I waited. I got more and more wound up. I cried. I got a headache. I asked for some tablets. "We have to ask the doctor before we can give you them," came the reply.

Eventually my solicitor arrived and the first question he asked me was, "Did you hit the man?"

"I can't remember. I don't know," I said, pleading ignorance. By this time, I knew I had done something but I was not sure if I had actually hit anyone. Could I really have been so bold as to attack the burger man? My time in the cell had muddled my head. "Well, if I did hit him, he deserved it," I admitted eventually. "It's not funny living next to that smell; you wouldn't like it."

And the solicitor winked at me: "Well, you've taken on three men today."

"Yeah? Really?"

He winked again. "I've talked to the police and they're willing to let you off with a caution if you admit what you've done."

"Right." I just wanted to leave the station.

"The appropriate adult will be arriving soon."

This turned out to be a man, who sat while the policewoman inspector interviewed me. She kept asking me all these questions and I started to lose my temper.

"Just leave me alone and stop asking me all these questions. I'm fed up with this – I've been waiting ages and I've got a raging headache. I want to go home. That burger man should be in this room being interviewed, not me!"

And I started to go off on one again, because I was so angry with the man for having no planning permission and no toilet, and no hand washing facilitates... it was disgusting.

"We need to calm down a bit, Karen," said my appropriate adult. But I did not take any notice and the interviewer was not willing to listen to my ranting.

"We will pop you back in your cell, Miss Braysher, until we decide what action to take."

"I am NOT going back in any cell as it's making me ill, and you can't make me."

Thankfully, my appropriate adult insisted that I be allowed to wait with him in the waiting room while they made their decision.

Then they wanted to take my fingerprints and my photograph. You can just imagine the fuss I made; just like a child. "No, I won't. I refuse, and you can't make me!" Eventually, I listened to my appropriate adult who told me to calm down, and stop making myself ill. "We know you're not a criminal, but you must just do this for the police and then we can all go home."

Of course, I had to have the last word as they started to ink my fingers: "I don't understand what I'm doing this for, and I don't agree with it!" But then came the real crunch – I had to sign the charge sheet.

"I did not BEAT three men!" I shouted after reading the description of the crime. I was standing at the charge counter and they were wanting me to sign this bloody thing. "I'm not signing it. I don't agree with the word 'beat' or 'beating'."

"Yes, madam, but that is what the law states you did. I cannot put anything else down."

"Just sign it," sighed my solicitor, clearly getting tired of the whole episode.

In the end, I did sign it but wrote: 'Under duress. Karen Braysher.' My short trip to the station actually lasted over nine hours.

To round the story off, the next day I was still manic and very unwell, but I managed to put in a counter claim against the burger man saying that he had been homophobic towards me and Alison. We were interviewed at home by another lady officer and later given protection by a Community Police Officer every time there was a football match. Dr Dingelstad wrote a letter to the Council saying that I, his patient with a severe mental illness, should not be made to live next to this van as the risk of another manic episode was high. The burger man disappeared. Now no one at the train station, nor the fast food vendors cross me. They think I am terrible, but it is just my illness. I cannot help it and I can now see why Dad beat me so badly – he lost control, as I did.

Most of the time, my bipolar is now tamed. I know the monster is there, but I have my medication, my cat, my garden and I have my spiritualism where I can find peace of mind. I understand that I was genetically pre-disposed to bipolar and the kicks to my head 'switched' it on. I live with it. It is part of who I am. I deal with it.

# SAYING GOODBYE

THE greatest gift that you can leave the earth is your children – they carry not only your genes, but your thoughts and feelings. But, of course, I do not have that gift to leave. Instead, I had to find peace in my soul for my lost children and I also had to find other gifts to leave behind. Working through this process, these past two years, has been both cathartic and uplifting.

The healing began when I became absolutely irate on behalf of an Italian lady with bipolar who had come to Britain in 2012 for a training course. She had suffered from a panic attack connected to her stopping her regular medication due to pregnancy. The local health trust in the UK won a court order for the birth to be carried out by caesarean section and the baby girl was then taken into care and later adopted. I became manic about supporting this woman – I was on a crusade because I felt this woman's pain. How dare they take the baby away from her – if she had been on her tablets she could have had a baby like Lorraine.

I was telling one of my hairdressing clients, who is Catholic, about the case as she was a member of the charity LIFE. LIFE provides support for pregnant women who want an alternative to abortions, which they feel pressured to have. "What is LIFE doing about this Italian woman?" I ranted.

"I don't know anything about the case," she said. So, I proceeded to tell her all about this poor Italian lady.

"Karen, you know what," said my client, "you're not angry about the woman from Italy, you're angry for yourself."

"What…? Oh, rubbish."

"No, I mean it. You had your babies taken from you and you haven't dealt with that."

I stopped dead, scissors in hand, mid-snip. She was right.

"Why don't you spend a weekend at Rachel's Vineyard?"

"What's that?" I asked. I soon found out. It is a healing weekend where women (and men) who have experienced the trauma of abortion meet and support each other. The retreat I attended was at The Friars, in Aylesford, run by the Order of Carmelites. It was here I was able to confront my buried feelings. Rachel's Vineyard facilitated the learning and so many tears were shed that weekend by the whole group.

The first step was writing my 'angry letter' to Lynn (my original dyslexic attempt has been edited below):

*"Dear Lynn*

*I loved you very much at the time – I looked up to you being 13 years older than myself. I am more than disappointed that your throw-away attitude influenced my decision to have an abortion and then to have the second abortion 1 year later.*

*I am angry that you put my whole future at risk and the physical termination of my two children to the forefront of our relationship. In my 'vulnerable state', having an undiagnosed mental illness and the recent loss of my father, you influenced my mind by threatening to leave me – which you did in the end anyway. Each relationship from there on has had that familiar pattern. If I had not listened, the physical presence of my children would be a comfort, as perhaps blood is thicker than water."*

By acknowledging my deep anger towards Lynn, I was able to then properly forgive her and it is interesting that I saw the pattern which had developed in subsequent relationships. Forgiveness allowed me to accept what Lynn (and my mother) had done, but also to reconcile the loss of my children.

I then went on to write a letter to Lilly and Sebastian, which I read out during the memorial service at the end of the weekend:

*"Lilly – you were conceived on a beautiful day in a foreign land – on a stunning beach. Your father and I met on a brief encounter. I imagine you are a beautiful woman by now. I have had confirmation that 'Daisy' my maternal grandmother brought you up in the spirit world. I have always had you in my thoughts and you will continue to always be close in my heart. If you ever find it appropriate to give me a sign that*

*you walk with me, I shall be glad to receive your communication. Until we meet in the spirit world, I will leave you in the hands of our great family, guided by God.*

*Sebastian – my son – I have always loved you and know that you are a great strong man now. I know that you are with me and protect me from evil. I thank you.*

*Your father and I miss you, and have always done so. I know that 'Daisy' my maternal grandmother has brought you up with lots of love. And as various aunties, friends and relations pass over to the spirit world, you have become a guide.*

*Your grandfather – Reginald Braysher – has been with you from the start and I know that you have enjoyed his practical help and guidance.*

*Please make yourself known to me if it is appropriate to do so – I will hear your sign. Walk tall beside me. Until I pass over, look after your sister, Lilly, and I am looking forward to you meeting me in the spirit world. Love Mum."*

As you can see from the letter, my spirituality had blossomed. I was, by then, attending many group circles. Spiritualism gave me (and still gives me) a sense of peace and it is often the way that people with bipolar will become fixated on religion. My religion, now, is a mix of Spiritualism and Church of England and I find so much relief in thinking of my children beside me and waiting for me.

The memorial service was the highlight of the retreat as it gave me, and all the other people gathered there, the feeling of not being alone. And the memorial service provided us with a dignified and proper send-off for our children which we had never had. It legitimised our children – they became real flesh and blood and allowed us to grieve freely, without restrictions.

I said my goodbye to Lilly and Sebastian. I also did not feel alone any more.

But that was not the end of my healing because I made two vows for my future. Firstly, I was so struck by the number of women in a similar position to me – there were 15 at the retreat – and I realised, after looking at the internet, that no research had been done, specifically, on the psychological effect of the earlier abortion in later life, especially after menopause. I was struggling with the impact of my abortions 30 years or so after the event, and I was absolutely sure that others would be too. I pledged to create a formal research proposal to highlight the need for a PhD-level research study so that women in the future could be provided with information relating to the long-term emotional impact of having an abortion. When I think back to my abortions it makes me so angry when I realise how little information I was given, and how my 'right to choose' was taken away from me as I was only given the 'benefits' of getting rid of my babies. Perhaps I would have made a different decision if I had been armed with balanced facts.

I also made a new commitment to the retreat group, before we all left: "I'm going to try and adopt," I told them.

"Hear, hear," came the reply from my newly-found supporters.

I started off being interviewed by an adoption agency in 2014 as my bipolar was under control and Alison had left my life. Now was the time to give a child a new life, as I had been given mine. There was no age restriction and they were fine with me as a single parent. I had my own home, with no financial worries, so I thought I was the ideal candidate. My adopted child would get everything I had worked so hard for.

The social worker from the London agency spent two hours with me and at the end of our meeting she turned to me and said, "You haven't got any chance whatsoever of adopting."

"Why?!"

"Because of the bipolar, and the fact you are on statins and have a thyroid condition. You don't have a hope in hell, and I'm so sorry to tell you that. You can go to other agencies if you like, but the answer will probably be the same. I won't be taking your case any further."

At the time I was deflated, but I became angry when I received the letter stating the main reason for my not being able to adopt was my bipolar. But there was no real fight left in me. I am obviously not meant to have children in my life, I thought. Perhaps it is for the best though, with the leakages I have, would I be safe with a child?

I finally had to put any thoughts of having a child to bed and shut the door.

However, a few weeks later I started to form an idea which has led to my full healing and given me closure where children are concerned. When I was re-cutting the hair of the lady who recommended I go to Rachel's Vineyard, we were talking about the retreat, and about the adoption fiasco when it suddenly dawned on me. I could leave this house to LIFE. I could leave it to all those homeless pregnant woman as a safe house.

I called the charity after careful consideration and arranged for them to visit my home so I could see if they thought it suitable to leave in trust to LIFE. As soon as they looked round the house they agreed to my offer. I felt absolute peace because I knew that my life had not been a waste. My house would be used to help women who were in my position all those years ago. And LIFE suggested the house be called 'Lilly & Sebastian Cottage' – it is as though my children gave their lives to help other children and young women. When I am gone, I can look down from the spirit world and say that I have given life to lots of babies, who would otherwise have been aborted – as mine were. My head will be held high. "What more can I do in the circumstances?" I said to Caroline, the solicitor I have asked to execute my will. "I have no children to my name, even though I tried so hard, and yet now, just think, babies could be born in my house. What a positive legacy that is."

Karla and Fleur, my nieces, are/will be Trustees of 'Lilly & Sebastian Cottage' and I hope that they will continue to allow LIFE to use my home when I am long gone.

With my physical wealth safely in trust for future generations – known, and unknown, to me – my thoughts naturally turned to getting the abortion research study off the ground.

In 2009, I was elected as Service User Governor of the Brighton & Hove constituency of Sussex Partnership NHS Foundation Trust. This was a position which I felt gave me influence as a user of NHS mental health services, so I could help make changes to the way those with mental health issues, learning difficulties and drug/alcohol problems are treated in the community and in hospitals. It also gave me a platform to prepare and propose a 'position paper' which could be taken up by university researchers. And, as I write this book, the formal position paper is finished and is being circulated amongst the universities, trying to marry-up with a researcher. My aim has always been for my generation to find support and acknowledgement for their suffering and to enlighten future generations about the long-term emotional impact of abortions.

# CAMPAIGNING FOR ACCEPTANCE

MY main focus as a Governor within the NHS Trust is to help those currently battling with diagnosed, and undiagnosed, bipolar. I am adamant that my experiences will not be repeated. I want to increase awareness of bipolar to aid early diagnosis and campaign for GPs to refer repeatedly depressed young people to secondary care as a matter of course. It is also important to educate the public about bipolar and to remove the stigma attached to mental illness. It is my calling in life: to play my part in creating a world where everyone is accepted, despite a physical or mental disability.

In the future, I will be battling for mental health assistance dogs to be licensed in the UK and this aim is purely based on my own experience where I felt a dog would have saved me from a whole heap of embarrassment and subsequent grovelling. Often in stressful situations I will make sudden comments or ask questions loudly, without any warning, and my dyslexia will cause me to stutter. I find pounding my fist on the desk, to beat out a rhythm, allows my words to flow better. However, only recently, I had a 'leakage' of bipolar during a Steering Group meeting, which was pretty terrifying.

There were many stressors leading up to, and during, the meeting and I did not have a mentor with me (mentors are not available during off-shoot meetings). Usually this person would have stopped me from getting too 'excited' and would have calmed me down, but I had no one there to prevent me from having an outburst. It was not an ordinary show of emotion either, because I was mortified by my behaviour which was 'off the wall' and plain rude. Something came over me that I had never experienced before: a loud, monotone 'voice' came out of my mouth. It scared me, and everyone present. I was described as 'hostile, aggressive and intimidating' by those who were in the room – which was fair comment.

The next day I was so overwhelmed by my behaviour that I called on my psychiatrist for reassurance. I wrote in my 'Learning Outcomes' report, following the incident (edited for clarity):

*"An episode of bipolar affects me every time it happens. It goes on for weeks after the event. It upsets other people. It gets me into trouble and gives me a bad name. I find the whole thing embarrassing and awkward. It could have been avoided."*

My outburst was caused by stress because many normal 'reasonable adjustments' put in place during meetings were not evident. As a service provider, under The Equality Act 2010, any association, club or society should make provision for people's disabilities – in the case of bipolar this could be paying particular attention to providing full and correct information, introducing everyone at a meeting, understanding direct, forceful speech is part of the makeup of bipolar and making allowances. However, even though I felt provoked into an outburst, I knew I had to later apologise to all concerned and I removed myself from the Steering Group, as without a mentor I felt 'unsafe' to continue.

But, on reflection, why should I have to curtail my Governors' role and effectively discriminate against myself? I recognise that having a mentor in every meeting is both expensive and a heavy use of resource, but a dog by my side would allow me not only to fully interact within the NHS, but also in society and other business events.

I do not recognise when I am having a bipolar episode and there is nothing I can do to stop one occurring. The dog would 'tell' me when I was about to have a manic episode (they would recognise the signs of anxiety) and would guide me (by pawing or nuzzling me) to take action to remove myself from the situation before I made an embarrassing, horrendous gaff. A service dog would give me a lifeline, as they do for physically disabled persons. A mental illness is a disability, just one often hidden from view. I will be very vocal in my support of Government acceptance for the need for bipolar dogs – and psychological assistance dogs, in general.

I have already done some fighting on behalf of people with bipolar. I had a run-in, in 2015, with a local women's business group and it was not a pleasant position to be in. Bipolar is just not understood. The Chair of the group had phoned me to tell me I was not welcome to further meetings because of my 'repeated disruptive conduct during meetings', even though I had made them fully aware of my bipolar and dyslexia. There was no understanding, just unkindness and no 'reasonable adjustments' were made for me. A solicitor's letter soon reminded them of their duties under the Equality Act and a refund of membership was given, but the personal nature of the attack made me feel suicidal, and if my lodger had not been in the house at the time of the phone call, I could easily have gone over the edge.

I appreciate that people see me as rude and probably combative, but that is just my illness (and my personality as well). I hope that the group concerned will take their responsibilities towards the disabled seriously in future, rather than just deciding that I was a personality which did not fit into their group. And while I wish I did not have bipolar, there are also positive aspects to being bipolar which I would like to share.

As I have already said, bipolar people are very creative and when 'on form' can inspire and lead people – think of Winston Churchill, for example. When I am positive, I can achieve anything I put my mind to, even if I am told I will never succeed: I go out of my way to exceed expectations. The following two stories are examples of my 'manic achievements':

When I was first elected in 2009 as a Governor, I found my much needed 'role model' in the form of an inspirational pioneering psychiatrist called Dr Helen Boyle. Dr Boyle put Brighton and Hove on the map of mental health history in the early 1900s. As I uncovered more about her, I felt drawn to her because she, too, had fought the stigma of mental health albeit from the opposite direction.

She had started off, in Brighton, as a GP and then worked in a dispensary for women and children who could not afford GPs' fees. Eventually, her calling came when she began taking women with fledgling nervous and mental disorders, from the poorest areas, and rather than not treating them and allowing them to be certified as lunatics in the asylum, she opened Aldrington House to provide holistic treatment to help them recover while they were still able. Depressed, neglected and exhausted women were treated in the 10-bed unit – called The Lady Chichester Hospital for Women and Children with Nervous Diseases – and given a range of treatments, including electrical therapy, hydrotherapy, massage, relaxation and psychotherapy, and they enjoyed the sea air and coastal sunshine. She continued her revolutionary, and highly successful, work for 50 years, until the unit was taken over by the NHS.

Yet, despite her incredible work, there was no formal record of herself, or her work – so I set about getting a Blue Plaque installed on Aldrington House, with a panel of information about her in the building. Most people laughed when they heard my plan.

In September, 2015, I helped unveil the Blue Plaque on Aldrington House – I had achieved what many others thought impossible, but there was no way, on my crusade, I would fail to honour Dr Helen Boyle and, believe me, I had to walk through treacle to achieve this.

I will carry on campaigning to have the house, which now houses NHS administration offices, turned back into a 'community half-way house' where those with mild mental health issues can be treated, and those coming from a secure hospital can readjust to life before being turned out into the community. There are such 'Crisis Houses' in Hastings and Horsham, and Brighton & Hove needs one. There is real demand for this holistic approach to return – sometimes the best answers are from the past. People might not live in such appalling conditions as in Dr Boyles' time, but modern drudgery exists in work, paying bills and fighting addictions.

I have to say here that without my mentors, I would have been lost. They are all powerful, strong women, who have been on my side pushing for me to be heard and inspiring other people's confidence in me. They have stopped me when I needed to be held back in meetings and I have listened to them because I have respected and trusted them. It is true to say that if I did not have such mentors then my voice, and enthusiasm, would be lost. And although in the letter below, one of my mentors, Melloney Poole OBE, gives me all the credit for getting the Plaque in place, I could not have achieved it without her support. Melloney sent me this lovely letter when she had to retire from the Foundation Trust:

*"I really wanted to say how much I valued knowing you and how much I admire your determination, commitment and courage. It has been a great privilege to work with you. You bring so much to your role as a Governor and are behind many of the changes that have resulted in better care. I'm really sorry not to be around for the plaque ceremony. You and you alone got that done... I shall miss our meetings and shall often think of you as one of life's enhancers. You are quite simply a star. With great affection..."*

Even though I am proud of getting Dr Boyle's Plaque commissioned, the proudest moment in my life was when I watched from the wings as my sister, Lorraine, was presented at Windsor Castle to Princess Anne on 25th November 2015 as 'Lorraine Mercer, MBE'. I had spent many 'manic' months getting the paperwork together and filling in online forms to nominate my sister for the award – with plenty of help from my 'intelligent' friends – because I felt she deserved recognition for her increasing charity work. Lorraine already had her Gold *Blue Peter* badge (awarded to extraordinary adults inspiring the nation's children), for her visitor work with the chaplaincy team at the Princess Royal Hospital, and she had carried the Olympic Torch in 2012 through Crowborough, but when I saw her collecting money outside Sainsbury's for her favourite charity, Riding For The Disabled, she looked so vulnerable and unhappy that I decided I should try to help elevate her charity work. I wanted people to know that she mouth-painted landscapes/buildings and turned them into charity cards. I wanted people to know that she inspired people when they were recovering from strokes and finding it hard to regain their ability to walk. I wanted people to know that Lorraine told no one (not even me) about the amount of charity work she did.

When she was called forward, and I saw her nervous and worried expression change to one of elation, I could not have been more excited for her or happier. When we watched the BBC *Six O'Clock News* that evening, surrounded by Lorraine's carers and friends at our hotel, it was my sister who was featured in the news segment, not the well-known celebrities. It was Lorraine as a Thalidomider who grabbed the headlines – disabled, yes, but never giving up and working for the good of others. That is Lorraine's legacy.

Unfortunately, our mother was not in the least bit interested in Lorraine's MBE and when I showed her photographs of the day she looked at them for a few seconds, said, "Yeah, very nice," and handed them back to me. She turned down my offer of framing a photograph so she could hang it on her wall and, to be honest, that was the final nail in the coffin for me. There are also members of the family who have not even congratulated Lorraine.

There are many disabled people in society (with less obvious disabilities than Lorraine) who are also not treated with respect – mainly because of the continued stigma attached to mental and physical illness. It is perhaps hard to see past people's exterior, but you should never judge a book by its cover because there are surprises lurking beneath, if you can unlock them. Sometimes it is hard to engage with people and it takes effort to find a common language, but there are huge rewards when a connection is made. Take, for example, my experiences as a community hairdresser: giving those with learning difficulties a decent haircut, not a cranky-looking fringe, when they ask using body language. Or singing old show tunes to those with Alzheimer's as you cut their hair. Respect for the individual.

I also hope to see a time, very soon, when it is perfectly normal for a person with less obvious physical disabilities (like mine) to be working in the community and our special analytical, artistic and creative skills to be seen as gifts. I once saw a presenter at a Bipolar UK conference (I am a co-facilitator for the Lewes branch) say that bipolars should wear a badge saying, 'Lucky for you, I'm bipolar' and I completely agree with that. My two careers – music and hairdressing – have actually worked very well for me, as has being self-employed (because I do not like being told what to do). With service dogs by our side, the world would be open to receive the benefits being bipolar brings.

# SEARCHING FOR JUSTICE

THE idea of writing this book initially seeded itself as a way of recording my life so that future mothers using 'Lilly & Sebastian Cottage' would understand who I was and why I had left my house to LIFE.

I also thought that writing about my experience of undiagnosed bipolar might help speed up detection in people who identified with my account, as Stephen Fry's documentary had worked for me. I also wanted to educate people about what it is like to live in the community with an undiagnosed, and diagnosed, mental illness. I have never been sectioned, so I have coped by soldiering along, experiencing ups and downs, brushes with the law, being hospitalised, repeatedly on the verge of suicide and contemplating failed suicides. I hope it has been an eye-opening account.

The process of unpacking my life, and seeing it written down in black-and-white has had a profoundly unsettling, yet ultimately healing, effect on me.

When I sat down with my ghostwriter, Hannah (I could never have written this without her help), back in January 2016, I had in front of me a large stack of photocopied notes which I had requested from my GP. These were my medical notes dating back to when I was at Chailey School and I had never seen the reports from the educational psychologist, the social worker nor the psychiatrist. It was shocking and eye-opening to read what went on behind the scenes, and it suddenly hit me that I had been lied to for all those years because, as I looked through the notes, there was the stark evidence of the physical abuse which I had suffered. I should explain that when I started to unravel my childhood with Suzanna Lobb (when I first realised that hitting children was a bad thing), I confronted my mother on several occasions. Each time she would say, "Oh, it wasn't that bad! You must have dreamt that you were being kicked in the head. What rubbish that woman's filling your head with." And, of course, I had believed my mother.

But now the social worker's report, especially, proved the reality of what life had been like at home – my father's anger issues and the aggressive/violent atmosphere which prevailed. Even though I knew the truth by now it was still a huge shock to see it confirmed on paper. My mother had told me a big lie – that I was crazy – to cover up what had happened. I used to have a regular dream, after Dad died, that he was actually in prison on a life sentence and rather than admit to me that Dad had done something bad, Mum had arranged this elaborate funeral and pretended he was dead. All I kept saying to my mother in the dream was, "Why did you not tell me the truth?" Perhaps I have never trusted my mother and, this year, I have proof that she lied about the extent of the abuse. I did not dream it – I was hit and kicked, viciously and repeatedly, in my teenage years.

The extent of the abuse explains why my father came to apologise to me back in 2000. I was on holiday with Pat in the Big Sur, a national park in California, when one night I believe I left my body. I was sat on the end of my bed and I visualised my father sitting on the end of Pat's bed. He was there in front of me. Peaceful, cross-legged and looking gentle – the opposite of the angry and ill man I had sometimes known. He spoke softly to me: "I'm sorry, Karen, for all the things I did to you."

"What do you mean?" I replied.

"I really need to apologise because what I did was wrong and I am truly sorry."

At the time I had no idea what he was telling me. What was he apologising for? He had beaten me, yes, but that was (I had been told by my mother) because I was naughty and deserved it; everyone got hit as a child.

It was only when I read the social worker's reports, 16 years later, that I realised what his apology had really meant and I could finally accept it. My mother, on the other hand, as the instigator and person who callously stood by and watched the abuse, has never apologised and I can see she never will. She is selfish, with some traits of narcissism; she will never see my perspective or accept that she did anything wrong.

I do not feel ready to talk to my mother about it because I cannot forgive her and I am likely to have a manic episode if I try. The whole realisation of being lied to has unsettled me and I have had to ask for an increased dosage of medication. I do not want to upset, or shout at, a frail, old lady, so I am protecting her by not seeing her. My siblings think I am just 'bad' for not seeing her. Anyway, if I did confront her she would phone my brother and sister and tell them that I had been 'naughty' again. This would cause them to call me to tell me off and this is a pattern I do not want to repeat. I am now 54 and too old to be repeating the same old mistakes.

I now feel emotionally healed in many ways: about my abortions, about my inability to have children and my father's actions. These things no longer haunt me. However, I feel I still deserve some justice. Some acknowledgement that these things happened to me and badly affected my life.

When I realised the extent of the abuse I suffered, I went to Victim Support to see what could be done for me. They asked me what I felt I had lost out on in life. I answered, "Goodness only knows what the physical abuse did to my brain – perhaps it 'switched on' my bipolar, as I was probably carrying a predisposition to mental illness from my father's side of the family. Perhaps the beatings also contributed to my dyslexia? And to the problems I have with my blurred/double vision? I lost out on my education – stunted; I did not marry the man I loved because I could not stand up to my mother – stunted – and did not have the children I conceived because I could not stand up to Lynn – stunted."

Although I have done well in life that is in spite of the abuse, rather than because of it. Nothing good has come from the abuse and with my father gone there is no one to answer for the crime. The only option open to me, which I am now pursuing, is through the Criminal Injuries Authority (based in Scotland) who are investigating to see if there is a crime to answer for. They will look at medical records, school records and social worker reports which are held internally, and those should provide further unseen evidence of abuse. If there is enough evidence of a crime, then I will get compensation from the Government.

But it is not the money I am after. I would do anything to have my children now, rather than money. I am looking for justice. For recognition that I have lost out because of the abuse. It has had an impact on my life – you only need to look at brain injuries sustained by boxers to realise that repeated bashes to the head cause problems in later life. But my older siblings and mother do not seem to realise this.

I am compliant, in terms of taking my medication, so that I can get along in society and not be a burden on anyone. I am financially solvent and I look after myself. It is easy to think that I am fine because I do not now make a fuss – but that is because I have been told not to make a fuss. My bipolar is never discussed by my older siblings – it is an embarrassment, a taboo subject. I would say it was an inconvenient truth, but I do not even think that my family (except Lorraine) accept that my bipolar exists. I am still 'difficult' and 'naughty' Karen. They do not recognise (or do not seem to) that I have lost out big time in life due to the abuse I suffered. It is easy for them to say that there is nothing wrong with me now, but they are not in my shoes.

Lorraine knows the truth; but then Lorraine has received compensation for her disability. It is obvious to the outside world that she has lost out in life. It is not so obvious in my case – the problem with a relatively invisible disability.

But while my family support is limited to Lorraine, I have a wide network of professional help, mentors, friends and support groups, such as Bipolar UK, who keep me grounded and stable and I thank you all.

APRIL 2016

PART III AFTERWORD - THE HEALING

# REELING HEAD, STOPPED

WITH the book finished, in April 2016, I was left unfulfilled. The book was intended to leave behind my story, mainly focusing on my bipolar and the way it had affected my life. But I had not reckoned on how life-changing getting all my experiences down on the page would be.

It had opened a whole can of worms. Now, my world was rocked by the medical and social worker reports that had come to light showing parental abuse – the abuse I thought had happened, but had repeatedly been told had not. Now I knew it to be true and my brain went into overdrive, analysing life events and outcomes connected to the abuse. Several issues, in particular, sat there unresolved – glowering at me, making me angry.

The main thing burning in my brain was my search to find more documents about my abuse from East Sussex County Council. I wanted more background details, to add to my medical notes and my parents' letters. I was looking for: school records, police files, further Social Services records and my father's original letters to his MP. But, can you believe it, after months of internal requests, formal complaints, letters to my MP and anything else I could think of, there are no files. They have 'gone missing' or are 'lost'. I have exhausted every avenue.

My mind never rested and I could feel myself starting to get depressed and dangerously angry, so I went to see my psychiatrist. Was I suffering from a form of post-traumatic stress disorder? I had films repeating in my head of being beaten up, reliving the unfairness of it all, the things that were taken away from me, poor Lorraine's treatment and my older siblings not believing me.

How could I beat these demons? I was determined to conquer these thoughts; they were not going to ruin the rest of my life. I first had to heal the memories of abuse.

One night, I was wide awake and in desperation I phoned the Samaritans. I was not really sure what I wanted to tell the lady who answered, but when I told her about the abuse, both physical and emotional, she pointed me towards NAPAC, which is a charity for survivors of childhood abuse. Looking on their website, I found another charity called Heal For Life Foundation. They offered a five-day residential course aimed at healing the survivors of childhood trauma and abuse and I thought it was just what I needed. To get away and explore the abuse and its consequences.

In September 2016, I packed my bags and took the train to reach this manor house near Basingstoke, Hampshire. As I was being driven down the two-mile long drive, I started to have reservations. I was being locked away from the world for five days, I had to give them my mobile phone and I really had no idea what was going to happen, apart from it being a guided programme of healing with facilitators who were survivors of abuse.

It was nervous apprehension which greeted me in the lounge at the opening talk. We were all unsure, noticing the teddy bears which adorned the sofas and the colouring pens and stickers laid out to decorate our name tags. It was all a bit creepy, but obviously necessary if they were going to regress us to childhood. We found out about each other, briefly, and were told the main rule: if you got up to leave the room, you did not have to explain, you could just leave and someone would follow you. My group was mainly women in their twenties who had suffered sexual childhood abuse – they were lucky to have found this healing course at a young age.

The five days were very structured, with time for meditation, personal reflection, group activities and daily chores. These chores were interesting because you could choose what you wanted to do and you were helped with them, and thanked for doing the work. It was weird to be told to be careful when using a sharp knife in the kitchen, or that you were doing a great job of sweeping the fire grate. They were rewriting childhood memories: I used to have the dish towel thrown at my face and told to do the drying up. It was quite a carry on and there was hardly ever a please or thank you back then.

Another activity, after a guided meditation, was to draw pictures using our non-dominant hand. Unconscious images would be transferred to paper and mine always contained my mother. She was either faceless (except for her mouth) and bodiless (with just her clothes making up her figure), standing resolutely between Lorraine and me [as seen on this book's cover], or it was of her face, scowling, with her hair covered by the dreaded headscarf. She always wore it when she was in a bad mood and I knew when she put it on I would be dragged around the shops. I can remember asking her not to wear it. We had to burn these drawings, but I wanted to keep hold of them because they were pretty good and I wanted to have a record of them. In the end, I drew flames engulfing my mother, just so she could burn forever more in the pictures. That seemed an appropriate compromise to me.

During the days it was evident when others were having 'breakthroughs' in their healing as they left the room, followed closely by a facilitator. You might hear shouting and sobbing, but not the memories which were being faced. I was waiting for my emotions to explode, but I was actually quite calm until I was confronted with the news of a party.

We were all issued with invitations, like little kids. I thought it odd, but played along. At the party there were big boxes of dressing up clothes, which the facilitators started to put on, and lots of silly games to play, like pass the parcel. Again, I joined in – what was the harm. Then we were invited to go through to the tea party. It was supposed to be lunch, but the huge table was filled with bags of children's crisps, chocolate biscuits and bowls of sweeties; heaven for five year olds. I just could not face it.

It was in the lounge that I broke. I became very, very sad.

"Not only haven't I had these parties for my children, but this would be the time in my life where I would be helping at my grandchildren's parties, with my son or daughter. I'm missing out on grandchildren as well. I'm 54 and facing an empty nest, for the rest of my life," I said out loud.

It all bounced in my mind and I marched, in a deep fury, out of the front door. "What's the matter?" asked the lady who had followed me, obviously there to help me deal with the emotions which engulfed me.

'And who is to blame for that, Karen?" she asked after I had told her about my sadness.

"Well, I suppose I am in some way because I had the abortions."

"But why did you have the abortions?"

"It was Lynn, my girlfriend, who coerced me into it. She was 13 years older than me and didn't want children in her life."

The conversation changed direction to why I might have turned to Lynn in the first place.

"Was she a replacement mother?" asked the lady.

"Yeah, I suppose so."

"So who is to blame then, Karen?"

"Well, it's my mother then. She's inside my head all the time."

"Why don't you tell her that now?"

I was bemused. "She's not here," I said, surveying the sweeping lawns and parkland before me.

"Tell her. Tell her, now!"

So I did. I shouted so loudly, it was unbelievable. Swearing and everything. I was sweating and trembling with anger. "You fucking cow. How dare you fucking do that to my head? You've absolutely played with my head. How fucking dare you." It was the realisation that she had got into my head, like a worm, and made me do such stupid things, with desperate repercussions. Like saying goodbye to Adrian. Aborting two children. Playing up at school so I failed to get an education.

It was the first time that I had really blamed someone else for what had happened to me. Before I had always blamed myself for being weak, confused, ill, a bad person. Now I could see I could really blame my mother – her behaviour towards me had marked my life, even when she was not physically there. It was a revelation.

I followed the lady back into the mansion, and only then realised that she was dressed as a Hawaiian hula girl. I smiled at the sight. Dressing up clothes hung limply on the sofas in the deserted lounge as I returned to pick through the leftovers of the sugary feast with the other residents.

"Nice day, isn't it, Karen." Forced normality reigned, once more.

The next session which enraged me involved writing on a whiteboard the worst thing that anyone had ever said to you. Then you had to say that thing out loud and wipe it out and sit down. I was wondering what the hell to write down; then it came to me. My mother's stock statement. I wrote, very calmly: 'You were born with the cord around your neck, Karen. It's a pity it didn't strangle you at birth. I wish I'd never had you.'

I had never really analysed what those few sentences had actually meant. They were just throwaway lines to me, having heard them so often. When challenged, my mother would claim she was only joking. I had become anaesthetised to them. But as I was writing them down I could feel my anger rising and my voice quivered as I read them out. They were a death threat. It became crystal clear to me.

I wiped the stinging words away using the board rubber, "Well, you can FUCKING take it back," and threw it to the floor with such violence that it ricocheted off into someone's lap. "Take it back. I don't fucking care what you want. I'm here anyway and I am alive. Take it back."

A few seconds had passed but I felt utterly exhausted. I suppose it was the poison coming out of me; like squeezing a spot.

But there was still more poison to expel.

Although I had said my goodbyes to Lilly and Sebastian on the previous retreat at Rachel's Vineyard, talking about my abortions had brought deep guilt back to the surface. I might have realised why I had had the abortions – my mother had got into my head and driven me into the arms of Lynn – but I had the abortions so I was ultimately to blame. When I met with a facilitator, who's daytime job happens to be a vicar, for my one-to-one session I knew exactly what I was going to ask him. I got to my question after a bit of digression, but eventually I sobbed, "Does God hate me for the abortions I had?" Ultimately, I thought, if God could forgive me, then perhaps I could forgive myself.

The vicar knew my story already and he looked off into the distance and pointed to one of the mighty oak trees far away in the parkland. "You see that tree over there?"

"Yes."

"If I kicked the football we have been playing with this

afternoon as hard as your father kicked your head, it would take a period of time to reach the tree. Yes?"

"Of course."

"Karen, you have now reached the tree. Your head has been reeling all this time; it is no wonder you did silly things in that period of time. God knows this. Now you have reached the tree, and your head has stopped reeling."

And with that, he made the sign of the cross, "In the name of the Father, and the Son and the Holy Spirit, I absolve this woman of all guilt of abuse. In the name of the Father, and the Son and the Holy Spirit, I absolve this woman of all guilt of the abortions she had."

"Does God forgive me now?"

"Yes."

I cried. I cried like I had never cried before in all my life. It was from my very soul and it felt deep and magical. Cleansing. Making sense of suffering is healing, isn't it? I asked for a hug which was given and sealed the moment.

When I left the following day, just after lunch, we were all saying our heart-felt goodbyes and I became tearful. I had had such life-changing experiences during the retreat and it was hard to leave the security of that healing, supportive environment. Just then God sent me a sign. Above our head flew a kite, circling gracefully on the thermals, and I shouted, "It's a sign from God."

This guy with tattoos all up his arms asked me what the sign meant.

"Freedom. It's freedom."

As I was being taken to the station, I noticed one of my fellow male residents clutching a teddy bear (so he had something to cuddle back in the 'real world') and I thought of my own safety net, which was packed in my bag. It was a letter I had written to myself after a session about transactional analysis (TA). This letter has provided me with a tool to change my life. *The Games People Play*, the book by Eric Berne setting out TA, had been recommended to me by my old landlady, Asphodel, but because of my dyslexia I had not been able to access it. My take away point from the retreat was that in stressful situations it is easy for adults to slip back into child mode and become defensive. Adults behaving like damaged children. I can now see how my thinking, beliefs, feelings and actions have been shaped, especially, by my mother's treatment. I also realise that I never did have adults looking after me; I had two damaged people/children bringing me up (my mother herself was abused and had no counselling after Lorraine's birth, and Dad probably had undiagnosed anger and mental health issues). My parents were not equipped to be parents – I would get taken into care these days.

The facilitators asked us to write to 'our wonder child' – the child within us – after the TA session and here is what I wrote. It has been very important for me to understand that vulnerable child Karen is still inside me and I need to look after her. Bearing in mind my dyslexia, I think I come across remarkably clearly (my original letter has been edited for spelling):

*"Dear little Karen, you are special and a very clever and creative child.*

*Life is sometimes hard but I your adult am strong enough to deal with it. Everything is going to be okay.*

*I am going to nurture little Karen, and help her achieve all the goals she has set her sights on. When little Karen is afraid or has nasty words or deeds said/done to her – I am going to look after you in adult mode of thought.*

*I will never allow your honesty to be disbelieved – as I will guide you along with God's help.*

*I will help little Karen embrace fun and happy times.*

*I will love little Karen as she is wanted and appreciated. I am always here to listen.*

*Little Karen is accepted for who she is and is also taken seriously.*

*You are amazing and I am proud of you.*

*When little Karen cries it does not mean she is weak. You can trust that there will be no more lies.*

*You can be silly, but I will represent you in an adult way. You are free to make mistakes. If you are not included I will seek the reason why. If other family members try to hurt little Karen, I will keep little Karen away and instead treat little Karen to something really nice – like a trip to the movies.*

*I will always encourage little Karen to have the love of a Pet. I will always maintain this bond as Pets bring another dimension. And Pets bring unconditional external love.*

*Promises will not be broken and little Karen will not be disappointed – by myself the adult, as I will take time to explain things fully.*

*I will keep little Karen always under my wing of Love. I will honour and not under any circumstances allow any death threats, as I will send them back to the person who gave them, and not allow them to be minimalised.*

*If little Karen wants to be naughty and get messy, it's not your fault, and no blame will be given – I your adult will be here to help you.*

*You will never again be manipulated nor will little Karen be rubbished.*

*I will always be here for you.*

*Your adult."*

Since writing this letter I have, for example, stopped talking to my brother on the phone as he still denies that I suffered as a child from domestic violence. Adult Karen has made the decision to protect little Karen. I did not slam the phone down, or agree with him to keep the peace, but said, "I'm not putting up with this anymore. It is true, it did happen and if you're not prepared to believe me then I'm going to have to end this call." And I did.

My head is much clearer now, with regards to my family, and I have the tools to behave in a different way. I still have problems recognising when people are telling lies to me (after I was told never to tell lies, but repeatedly told lies by my mother) – I will have to learn some strategies to keep my promise to little Karen.

When I got home from the retreat, I felt relief that I had finally confronted the hurt of abuse and been absolved of my past mistakes (by the vicar) and now, having reached the tree, it was time for me to move on. I started to think about my personal situation. A few years ago, I had put myself in a protective bubble, scared to get hurt again. Now, desperately lonely, yet evolved from self-hate to accepting and respecting myself, I began to unpack what had gone wrong in my personal life. There was a pattern to my lesbian relationships: the desperate need and search for a mother figure, the masculine manic phase where I could take a lot on my shoulders and then the depression, and sometimes violent reaction, when the girlfriend gradually moved away from me. Each relationship, apart from Faye and Pat, crippled me emotionally and yet I repeated the same mistake again, and again. That was now in the past: lesbianism was a stage I went through and this leopard was going to change her spots.

It was back to my psychiatrist. "I want to make a male friend. I'm not thinking of some big sexual relationship. I'm just at this time thinking about a companion. But I don't feel I have the equipment to be able to do that."

Dr Dingelstad thought for a moment. He decided to take advice from the recovery team and psychologists at the hospital. The result was a course of Cognitive Analytical Therapy (CAT). I have had to tell my whole story to the therapist, which has been just as painful an experience as when I initially told my ghostwriter.

But I have learnt a few helpful things. I can see why, after Adrian's foiled rescue attempt to take me away from the abuse (by marrying me), I lost hope in a knight in shining armour (despite other boys' attempts) and instead turned to find comfort in the arms of a replacement mother. But I did not end up with the kind mother I was looking for, but a succession of women showing their true, messed up, colours – often suffering with their own problems. But it was just that abusive, domineering and controlling behaviour that kept me with them as it was actually a comfortable environment for me as I was used to this pattern of living, having had plenty of practise with my mother. I was not a lesbian at all; it was an escape route. I loved Adrian (and still think about him), but the women were the best option I had.

Is is possible, I thought eventually, that I got stuck in a time warp, at 17, when I finished with Adrian? Was I so damaged as a teenager by the unfairness and tragedy of my lost love that I could not move on with other men? Writing that letter under the watchful, piercing eyes of my mother; being marched to Adrian's door to deliver it by hand; trying to phone him to explain it was not me who had written it. Do I have to pick myself up again, as Teenage Karen, and move forward from there?

The next step is to plan out my route to meet a suitable male companion. I have to learn new ways of thinking and stop acting as rebellious, stroppy Teenage Karen. Could I have the confidence to accept a loving and caring relationship, without finding it uncomfortable and strange? I have already welcomed two lovely male student lodgers into my home which is definitely a step in the right direction. My ultimate hope is to meet a man who already has children, so I can become part of a real family. My new cat, John, would very much be part of that new family!

To end this memoir with a nod to a positive future, I am reinventing myself. I am perfecting the new fashion cuts for a young male clientele (I am already experienced in regular barbering), so I can set myself up as a unisex hairdresser, and I have also begun training as a Spiritual Minister with The Spiritualist National Union, despite my bipolar and dyslexia. I passed my first correspondence course with 88% (with the assistance of spell check on the computer) and the next course will get me speaking in public. It will take quite a few years to be put forward for ordination, but hopefully I can work towards being an officiant in the meantime, so I will be able to do spiritual officiant work, such as going into hospices, hospitals and prisons. There is a real demand for Spiritualist officiants in my area and I feel I can turn my negative experiences in life into a positive resource for relating with others when they need to trust in someone and receive support.

I feel as though I have finally come out of a horrible dream and begun to walk again. I have hope, faith and belief that I can pull Teenage Karen forward in time to live a magical life. I have reached the tree. My head is no longer reeling.

Not only is my head clearer, but I am much healthier since October 2016 when I had a replacement heart valve fitted after an echocardiogram found a childhood heart murmur (linked to streptococcal infection from a tonsillectomy) had steadily deteriorated into a double-ended leaking mitral valve (into the lungs and heart), causing pulmonary hypertension. I had a life-threatening condition, without realising. I might have had shortness of breath, coughed a lot and been tired much of the time, but never did I think, as I sat with my ghostwriter retelling my life story five months earlier, that I could have dropped dead. I was lucky to make it through Healing For Life, too. The surgeon who saw me after I was out of anaesthetic said, "I don't know how you have been walking about. The valve was so prolapsed it had fallen to the bottom of the [heart] chamber and I literally had to scoop it out!"

I am now the proud owner of a shiny, new prosthetic valve, clean out of the box and I am extremely lucky to be alive.

Lorraine was absolutely wonderful while I was in hospital; she is now my named next of kin. Her carers brought her in four times, which was an incredible effort, and she had a word with the surgeon and with the ward sister when I was uncomfortable and in distress. She took charge. It made me realise what I missed out on for all those years when my parents were my next of kin. Lorraine, despite her disability, did everything for me. She was also the person I turned to when I felt severely depressed after the surgery (nobody had told me that depression often follows heart surgery) and she kept my spirits up, checking in with me every day. She is marvellous; the best sister.

I am sure, in a few years, I will look back on the writing of my life story with great satisfaction. I hope this book will help people with mental illness get a quicker diagnosis because they might recognise some of the things that have happened to me. I hope my story will also talk to those who have been abused as children, to women who are distressed about past abortions and to mentally ill people not allowed to adopt.

There is always hope and you must believe in yourself. Sometimes your spirit gets crushed and broken, but hope will keep it alive. You have to believe in your spirit, and the hope that it will regenerate. I think my spirit saved me. There is no other way to be, otherwise you will end up in a progressively downward spiral.

Dad gave me a gift and that was perseverance. My nan, Nellie, gave me the gift of kindness. It is so important to leave behind gifts to future generations and I am sure that my experiences, good and bad, have been given to me for a reason. I hope I have, and will have, fulfilled my calling.

We are talented and different; the good days and bad days shape our destiny.

FEBRUARY 2017

# EPILOGUE

SUE and David, my elder brother and sister, did not personally witness the abuse I received from my parents as they had already married and left home, effectively leaving me as an only child (with Lorraine institutionalised).

I remain disappointed that they, especially Sue, were convinced by our mother's word against mine and still refuse to believe me.

I would like to thank all those who supported me during the creation of this book:

JANE GANE

HANNAH SHERRIFFS

BERNIE NYMAN

CAROLINE ARMITAGE

LISA RODRIGUES CBE

BARONESS VALERIE HOWARTH

DR ELIZABETH LAMB GP

DR KAY MACDONALD

DR LEON DINGELSTAD

KAREN NICHOLLS

LUCY HUNTINGDON

HEAL FOR LIFE FOUNDATION

THE REVEREND RAVI HOLY

RACHEL'S VINEYARD

ALL MY READERS WHO HELPED SHAPE THE CONTENT

GILL O'DONNELL

# USEFUL ADDRESSES

**BIPOLAR UK**
Bipolar UK is the national charity dedicated to supporting individuals with the much misunderstood and devastating condition of bipolar, their families and carers.
**www.bipolaruk.org**

**SAMARITANS**
Freepost RSRB-KKBY-CYJK,
PO Box 9090,
Stirling, FK8 2SA
Helpline: 116 123 (UK)
**www.samaritans.org**

**LIFE**
The positive alternative to abortion.
**lifecharity.org.uk**

**BRITISH DYSLEXIA ASSOCIATION**
Helpline: 0333 405 4567
**www.bdadyslexia.org.uk/contact**

**HEAL FOR LIFE FOUNDATION**
The Heal for Life Adult Program is a 5-day residential program designed to help you heal from childhood trauma and/or abuse.
**healforlife.org.uk/**

**NAPAC**
Supporting recovery from childhood abuse
**napac.org.uk**

**RACHEL'S VINEYARD**
For general enquiries or further information regarding the healing weekends please contact: Rachel's Vineyard UK, St Joseph's, 20 Westgate, Wetherby, West Yorkshire LS22 6LL
**www.rachelsvineyard.org.uk**

Printed in Great Britain
by Amazon